Spiritual Warfare Now
Fighting for the Souls of Men

Frank Marzullo, Jr.

Except where otherwise indicated all Scripture quotations are taken from The *New King James* Version of the Bible. Copyright © 1979, 1980,1982, 1990, 1995, Thomas Nelson Inc.,Publishers.

Copyright © 2013 by Frank Marzullo, Jr.
All rights reserved.

Published by:
Christian Covenant Fellowship
1300 Weymouth Dr
Deland, FL 32720
386-736-2820 Fax: 386-736-2820
www.spiritualwarfarenow.com

Spiritual Warfare Now : Fighting for the Souls of Men
ISBN-13: 978-1-892363-27-5

Printed in the United States of America

Table of Contents

Chapters	Page
Cleansing the Vessel	7
How do you know if you need Deliverance	29
Identifying Demons and Work of the Flesh	51
Knowing your Enemy	69
Pulling Down Strongholds	96
Emotional Triggers	114
Demonic Nature in the Deeds of the Flesh	137
Repentance	166
Self-Deliverance	186
Levels of Spiritual Warfare	207

Acknowledgments

I would like to thank and acknowledge my sister Cynthia Reddy for the painstaking work of correcting grammar and arrangement of some sentences of this manuscript to help the thought flow more fluidly. She spent a great deal of time going over this material for the benefit of the reader.

I also want to thank my sister Nina Snyder who worked on the consistency in the spacing, scriptural references, and bold type from chapter to chapter and did the finishing work that needed to be done in order for this manuscript to look professional.

After an explanation of what I wanted the cover to look like, I gave the task of designing it to my Daughter Lee Ann Marzullo. And I thank her in designing the cover. I am more than pleased. This was indeed a family adventure.

Thank You Clark Winchester of Wish Work Media of Daytona Beach, Florida for finishing the work on the cover and giving it it's present look.

Also I want to thank my lovely wife, Jill Marzullo, for giving me the time alone with my thoughts so that the Body of Christ could be healed and delivered.

Frank Marzullo, Jr.

Fighting for the Souls of Men
Spiritual Warfare Now
Preface

If you are being drawn to the ministry of deliverance, you must be prepared with the tools of the ministry that the Holy Spirit provides as found in 1 Corinthians 12:4-11:

There are diversities of gifts, but the same Spirit. There are differences of ministries, but the same Lord. And there are diversities of activities, but it is the same God who works all in all.

But the manifestation of the Spirit is given to each one for the profit of all: for to one is given the word of wisdom through the Spirit, to another the word of knowledge through the same Spirit, to another faith by the same Spirit, to another gifts of healing by the same Spirit, to another the working of miracles, to another prophecy, to another discerning of spirits, to another different kinds of tongues, to another the interpretation of tongues.

But one and the same Spirit works all these things, distributing to each one individually as He wills. (NKJV)

According to these verses, the anointing of God falls on individuals in three ways: **gifts, ministries** and **activities (workings)**. A person may operate in any one or all three ways of anointing according to the nine manifestation of the Holy Spirit listed in the verses above.

A person who is drawn to the deliverance ministry

(casting out of demons) needs to identify if demons are present. That deliverance worker needs to have several tools of the Holy Spirit.

First he needs Wisdom. I have seen many fools rush in and start deliverance at the wrong time. Next, they also need to have Knowledge, Prophecy, and Discerning of Spirits to be fully mature.

Please note that it is the Holy Spirit who gives to each one individually as He wills but Paul instructs us to seek or desire the gifts in 1 Corinthians 14:1 *"Pursue love, and desire spiritual gifts, but especially that you may prophesy."* (NKJV). If you are drawn to a certain area, it is normal to desire those gifts that will be used in those areas. Paul stated that he wanted to visit the brethren and release something of the Holy Spirit to them. He said in Romans 1:11, *"For I long to see you, that I may impart to you some spiritual gift, so that you may be established"* (NKJV).

God uses men and women of God, ministers, elders and leaders of the church in the same way Paul was used to release or impart those things into our lives in the timing of the Holy Spirit.

Please join me this prayer:

"Dear Lord Jesus, it is my desire to be all that you want me to be. I therefore ask you to fill me with your Holy Spirit. In Luke 11:13, you say to us, "If you then, being evil, know how to give good gifts to your children how much more shall your heavenly Father give the Holy Spirit to those that ask Him!" Heavenly Father, I ask you to fill me with the Holy Spirit with the evidence of speaking in tongues and at the same time I ask that you release to me gifts, ministries and activities of the Holy Spirit to use as tools in my warfare against Satan and his demons. I ask that you release those gifts to me now in the name of Jesus Christ. Amen."

In the following chapters, I will present a teaching to the body of Christ on how to be spiritually healed, to become spiritually discerning, how to recognize demonic behavior within themselves and how to be delivered of evil spirits in Jesus' name. I have placed the casting out of evil spirits at the end of each chapter to accomplish this purpose.

Chapter 1
Cleansing the Vessel

Can a demon/evil spirit occupy a born again believer? This is one of the most asked questions. When dealing in deliverance, (the casting out of demons), many people believe that a born again Christian can not be occupied by demons, but they are misinformed. First let's look at what it means to be born again.

You may say to yourself, "I don't think I need deliverance from demons. After all, I am a born again Christian." The Bible says in 2 Corinthians 5:17:

Therefore, if anyone is in Christ, he is a new creation; old things have passed away; behold, all things have become new. (NKJV)

And so you argue, "I can't be possessed by the devil. I can't be possessed, because that requires ownership. And a born again Christian cannot be owned by the devil." The Bible term for possessed is not a real clear explanation, A better word to be used in scripture is "demonized".

Yes I agree 100%. A born again Christian can not be possessed. So the question is, can a born again Christian have a demon or be demonized? The answer is, Yes! A born again Christian can have anything he wants, and he can also be demonized.

The Bible tells us in 1 Thessalonians 5:23, we are made of body, soul, and spirit.

*"Now may the God of peace Himself sanctify you completely; and may your whole **spirit**, **soul**, and **body** be preserved blameless at the coming of our Lord Jesus Christ."* (NKJV)

Jesus tells us that the spirit of man is born again in

John 3:3-6:

Jesus answered and said to him, "Most assuredly, I say to you, unless one is born again, he cannot see the kingdom of God."

Nicodemus said to Him, "How can a man be born when he is old? Can he enter a second time into his mother's womb and be born?" Jesus answered, "Most assuredly, I say to you, unless one is born of water and the Spirit, he cannot enter the kingdom of God. That which is born of the flesh is flesh, and that which is born of the Spirit is spirit." (NKJV)

It is the spirit of man that is reborn-- made into a new creation. It is not the flesh (the body), nor the corrupt mind (soul), but that which is born again is the spirit of man.

And do not grieve the Holy Spirit of God, by whom you were sealed for the day of redemption. Ephesians 4:30 (NKJV)

This word proclaims that a believer is sealed for the day of redemption by the Holy Spirit. **Your spirit is sealed like a promissory note to God.** No demon can break into this area but they can go into other areas such as the flesh.

So the flesh (our body) and the soul (our mind, will and emotions) can be afflicted, harassed, oppressed, and controlled. This is where demons operate and take up their residence in born again Christians, in our bodies and souls and that is where the devil demonizes.

Family, Jesus said that which is born of the Holy Spirit is man's spirit. You see, it is your spirit that the Holy Spirit comes into and makes reborn. It is not your flesh or your soul, but your spirit that is reborn. An example of an evil spirit attached to the flesh is found in the book of Luke.

And behold, there was a woman who had a spirit of infirmity eighteen years, and was bent over and could in no way raise herself up. Luke 13:11 (NKJV)

And they could also attach themselves to the **soul of man**; also know as the **heart of man.** The **heart** mentioned here in the Bible is the representation of the **soul of man,** (your intellect, will, and emotions is your soul).

> Matthew 15:19-20 (NKJV) *For out of the heart proceed evil thoughts, murders, adulteries, fornications, thefts, false witness, blasphemies. These are the things which defile a man...*

> Mark 7:21-23 (NKJV) *For from within, out of the heart of men, proceed evil thoughts, adulteries, fornications, murders, thefts, covetousness, wickedness, deceit, lewdness, an evil eye, blasphemy, pride, foolishness. All these evil things come from within and defile a man.*

These things and more are already in the heart/soul of man and demons will attach themselves to these areas if allowed to help you accomplish what is already in your heart/soul to do.

An example of demons attached to the soul of man is found in: Acts 5:1-6:

> *But a certain man named Ananias, with Sapphira his wife, sold a possession. And he kept back part of the proceeds, his wife also being aware of it, and brought a certain part and laid it at the apostles' feet. But Peter said, "Ananias, why has Satan filled your heart to lie to the Holy Spirit and keep back part of the price of the land for yourself? While it remained, was it not your own? And after it was sold, was it not in your own control? Why have you conceived this thing in your heart? You have not lied to men but to God. Then Ananias, hearing these words, fell down and breathed his last. So great fear came upon all those who heard these things. And the young men arose and wrapped him up, carried him out, and buried him.* (NKJV)

Satan filled his heart. Heart and soul are interchangeable in the Word of God. They mean the same, the will, intellect, emotions. It is the person's mind, the way they think, that shows the condition of their soul as it did with Ananias.

So we know that demons can attach themselves to the flesh and soul of man, but not the reborn spirit of man. A good example of a spirit filled person who is afflicted by demons is King David.

Here is a person who is noted as "a man after God's own heart." He was anointed as a young boy to later be king and a righteous man filled with the Holy Spirit, but later in his life according to the Word of God in 2 Samuel Chapter 11 (read whole chapter), David was guilty of the sins of lust, adultery and murder. First he was filled with lust for Bathsheba when he saw her bathing on the roof. Next he sent for her and committed adultery with her. Then after she was found to be pregnant with his child, to hide his sin, David sent for her husband from battle so he would sleep with his wife; but out of loyalty to the king and his men he wouldn't sleep with her, then finally King David had him killed in battle.

David, man of God, Spirit filled man, but also filled with lust for another man's wife, an adulterer, and a murderer. David was undoubtedly led by demons to carry out these acts. Nathan the prophet came to confront him with his sins and he repented. We read that in anguish, David prayed to the Lord

> *Cast me not away from thy presence; and take not thy holy spirit from me. Restore unto me the joy of thy salvation; and uphold me with thy free spirit.* Psalm 51:11-12 (KJV)

The Holy Spirit who was in David never left him, and convicted him of his sins. I have met many Christians who are caught by some sin from the past or maybe, just lost their way. The first thing that leaves is their joy of salvation. David had evil spirits, demons of lust, adultery and murder that entered into him and caused him to sin and thus lose the joy of his salvation, his intimacy with the Lord.

It is very important to notice the wording of David's prayer. He asked God to restore to him the **joy** of his salvation and he asked God not to take the Holy Spirit from him. David lost his joy because of sin, but he never lost the presence of the Holy Spirit. God does not withdraw His Holy Spirit from believers even if they are afflicted with demons. David's behavior is scriptural evidence that the Holy Spirit can indwell a sinful vessel yet God does not take the Holy Spirit from him.

You and I are no different. Demons of evil thoughts can take up residence in our minds/souls and fill them with adulteries, fornications, lust, murders, thefts, covetousness, wickedness, deceit, sensuality, pride, foolishness, and all sorts of evil can fill the minds/souls, and actions of born-again Christians and at the same time the Holy Spirit indwells them. God in His mercy does not take His Holy Spirit from us when we sin.

So we can see that demons can indwell the flesh of man with physical sickness (spirit of infirmity) and we can see that demons can indwell the flesh, soul/heart of man with (spiritual sickness) wicked thoughts and actions.

I have seen Christians backslide and then the Holy Spirit calls them back in a relationship with the Lord and they start using their gifts again. The Holy Spirit never left them and their gifts never left. Maybe their gifts dried up for a season, but the gifts never left them because, *"the gifts and the **calling** of God are irrevocable."* Rom. 11:29.

Family, part of the way we keep our vessel clean is to occupy or to do business with what He gave us.

Therefore He said: "A certain nobleman went into a

far country to receive for himself a kingdom and to return. So he called ten of his servants, delivered to them ten minas, and said to them, 'Do business till I come. Luke 19:12-13 (NKJV)

Kingdom of God. But some do not use their gifts, some do not know how, some don't want to use the tools that Jesus left them to use, and do not use the gifts of the Holy Spirit because of fear of offending others.

As the story continues from verse 14 to 27 we find that the Lord takes the money/talent/gift away from those who didn't use it to produce. This is where I see the drying up of talents and someone else steps in place to produce what the Lord wanted produced. Even though the unproductive, wicked servant didn't produce, he still remained the Lord's servant, much like dried-up King David. As I have said before, many times I have seen dried- up people repent and restored and their calling was never revoked and God used them again for another task just as He did with King David. I have also noticed that if we don't occupy (do business) until He comes, we will be occupied by something other than the Kingdom of God. We will be occupied with the Kingdom of darkness to:

1. torment and afflict us.

2. To keep us from knowing Christ in all the ways He has redeemed us.

3. To keep us from serving Christ effectively

So, how do we know when we are being occupied? One of the ways is by how we view the wind. We never actually see the wind, but we see the effects of what the wind produces, dust being blown, leaves blowing down the street, trees and branches bending by the force of the wind. These are signs that there is a presence of wind. So it is with demons. We don't see them, but we can recognize their presence by certain actions.

The following is taken from the book "They Shall Expel Demons" by Derek Prince, Pg. 166 (not in the same order)

Demons entice, they harass, they compel, they enslave, they cause addictions, they defile, they deceive and they attack the physical

body, they torture.

1. Demons Entice by persuading people to do evil. Let's say that you find a woman's purse with her ID and a lot of cash in it and you are desperate for money at this time in your life and a voice inside you says take the money, no one will ever know. Everybody else does it. Don't be a fool and turn it in. And there you are, being enticed by an inner voice to do evil.

2. Demons Harass by following your movements, observe your weak movements, then engineer situations that will open up a way for them to slip in. Let's say you have a bad day and everything is going wrong. Your car won't start-dead battery, you change the battery and you're on the way to work, a bird poops on your new shirt when you get out of your car, there. You get in trouble with your boss at work, red lights and traffic all the way home. And you get home and your spouse says, "I just found a deal on an outfit and bought it. I need $200. Now this harassing demon has been working on you all day and that is it. Anger boils over, nuclear warhead missiles start to take off and you blow your top.

3. They Compel: Examples, smoking, alcohol, drugs, compulsive disorders, eating disorders, excessive talking

4. Demons Enslave: such as masturbation, fornication, adultery, homosexuality, perversions. People can't fully stop, they hate themselves for doing it and say, "never again," and then it happens again.

5 Demons cause Addictions.

Also here are some examples of addiction (taken from

"Walking the 12 Steps with Jesus Christ," by Ray Geisel pg.8 listing 30 common Addictions):

> alcohol, caffeine, the chase, (chasing after sex, pleasure, possessions) chronic illness, compulsive lying, obsessed with church, credit cards, other drugs-(illegal), emotional abuse, female dependency, addiction to prescription medication, physical abuse, pain, over eating, nicotine, money, male dependency, love(obsessive), gambling, fighting, sex, sexual abuse, shopping, Soap Operas, sugar, excessive talking, telephone, television, video games, work. There are many others not mentioned in this book.

What must be uncovered first and exposed is the underlying support of these addictions and the evil spirit that caused addictions must be cast out in Jesus' name. Some pain, emotional trauma, disappointment, mishap, or some wound is usually at the root of addictions.

I dig until I find out the cause of the pain, mishap or trauma, and then I cast out the evil spirit that came in by saying to the evil spirit, "You, the one that came in when such and such happened (and I name and describe the incident), "You come out in Jesus' name!"

> Paul writes to the Church in 1 Corinthians 6:12 (NKJV)
>
> *All things are lawful for me, but all things are not helpful. All things are lawful for me, but I will not be brought under the power of any.*

Paul stated that he would not be brought under the power of things. In other words, he would not be mastered by things. A person becomes addicted when they are brought under the power of anything and mastered by it.

6. Demons Defile; One main area they defile is our mental lives. Our thoughts and imaginations, impure thoughts, lustful images and fantasies project themselves on our minds. Strong impulses, profanity, blasphemy, and cursing are bi-products of defiling demons.

7. Deceiving Demons; 1 Timothy 4:1 (NKJV)

> *Now the Spirit expressly says that in latter times some will depart from the faith, giving heed to deceiving spirits and doctrines of demons,*

Family, Paul is telling us that these are Christians who will depart from the faith. They will have been deceived and enticed out of sound biblical faith into some form of doctrinal error (spiritual deception). Paul also warns that we can receive a different spirit and a different gospel of another Jesus if we receive false teachings.

> *For if he who comes preaches another Jesus whom we have not preached, or if you receive a different spirit which you have not received, or a different gospel which you have not accepted— you may well put up with it!* 2 Corinthians 11:4. (NKJV)

That different spirit is a deceiving evil spirit that changes and mixes different doctrines together to change what Paul teaches about Jesus.

8 Demons Attack the physical body; Illness, sickness, spirits of infirmities such as found in Luke 13:11-13.

> *And behold, there was a woman who had a spirit of infirmity eighteen years, and was bent over and could in no way raise herself up. But when Jesus saw her, He called her to Him and said to her, "Woman, you are loosed from your infirmity." And He laid His hands on her, and immediately she was made straight, and glorified God.*

Spirits of infirmity may not be a person bent double but they could cause people to be lame, blind, deaf, paralyzed, deformed withered and diseased.

9. Demons Torture. In Matthew 18 starting in verse 21 Peter asked Jesus about forgiveness and Jesus responds with a parable about a slave owing a lot of debt to his master and was forgiven and then grabs his fellow slave who owed him a little debt, but was unwilling to release him from that debt and threw him into prison. When the Master of the first slave heard about how unwilling he was to forgive his fellow slave, the master became angry and said to him in Matthew 18:32 (NKJV):

>…'*You wicked servant! I forgave you all that debt because you begged me. Should you not also have had compassion on your fellow servant, just as I had pity on you?*' *And his master was angry, and delivered him to the torturers until he should pay all that was due to him.*
>
> "*So My heavenly Father also will do to you if each of you, from his heart, does not forgive his brother his trespasses.*"

Family, I have found that there are various forms of being tortured. I have encountered many who are under emotional torture such as fear of some sort that would restrict their lives or bring insanity, and I have encountered many who have experienced physical torture by the enemy. Some who may have been sent there by the Father because of unforgiveness as mentioned above and some sent through their sins and ancestors sins (Ex. 20:3-5) Many physical illnesses such as arthritis, or diseases that twist and cripple are brought on by sins of unforgiveness or serving other gods.

I have prayed for many who seem to be under the torture of the enemy. The very first thing I do is lead them into repentance for their sins and ancestors sins, next, I lead them into **repentance** for their own sins especially for holding **unforgiveness** to another even if they think they have a right to hold a grudge. Then I loose or release the Kingdom of God for deliverance and healing. Here is one example;

I have experienced more people healed and more delivered for the Kingdom of God since I started to release **the Kingdom of God that is within me.**

Jesus said in **Luke 17:21**..*nor will they say, 'See here!' or 'See there!' For indeed, the **kingdom of God** is **within you.***"

Also, Paul proclaimed when speaking to the Colossians; "***Christ in you, the Hope of glory.***" **(Col 1:27).** We must remember that when we pray for anything, we pray from the position that Christ is within us as believers. And in Matthew 18:18 (NKJV)

*"Assuredly, I say to you, whatever you bind on earth will be bound in heaven, and whatever you **loose on earth will be loosed in heaven.***

A tormented woman was set free at our home church here in DeLand, Florida. This is how loosing/releasing *the **Kingdom of God within me (Christ within me the Hope of Glory)*** in deliverance first, then **loosing** and **releasing** of *the kingdom of God within me (Christ within me)* for healing next, brought healing to a lady who had **unforgiveness** and ancestral curses coming down the generational line for serving other gods. She had many illnesses and was in **great torment**.

She was a Christian lady who believed that Jesus Christ was her Lord. She had 6-7 major illnesses that could lead to death. I asked her a few questions about her family and found out that her parents were Chinese and their ancestors worshiped foreign gods. They became Christians and later moved to Jamaica and that is when she got involved in Santeria witchcraft to put a spell upon another person. Her sister and her brother-in-law stole the house and assets from her leaving her bitter and angry and her father was a Freemason.

I have also found that demons can enter a person through a gateway either from their fleshly appetites or because of their own sinful decisions or actions. Deliverance from demons is not fully accomplished until you locate the entry point or gateway, the door of entry.

I explained to her how her ancestor's worship of other gods made God jealous and this could have opened a door for a generational curse for demons to afflict (Ex. 20:3-5) and that could be the cause of her torture and illnesses. Next her father was a Freemason and took a Masonic oath which also could have caused her torture and illness since the god of the Freemasons is Lucifer; this could have also caused the same curse to fall on her. Next she opened the door to the occult through Santeria witchcraft which could have cursed her and could be the cause of her torture and illness, and last she held bitterness and unforgiveness toward her sister and brother-in-law which more than likely sent her to the tormentors, causing her torment and illness. *(Read Matt.18:34-35)*

When these things were explained to her, that these things could have caused her physical condition, a great sadness came over her and she tearfully repented and asked God to forgive her. I prayed the **"loosing and releasing of the Kingdom of God upon her"** and cast demons out of her in the name of Jesus and then I prayed **"the loosing and the releasing of the Kingdom of God upon her"** for her healing in the name of Jesus Christ. I called out evil spirits that caused her condition: unforgiveness, bitterness, hatred, idolatry, witchcraft and evil spirits that caused circulation problems hardening of the arteries, high blood pressure, Raynaud's syndrome.

Remember this, Family, when you pray in faith in the name of Jesus Christ, you must believe that what you have prayed for has gone forth and will be accomplished.

Her hands were dark purple, almost black, because of poor circulation due to these diseases. They were ice cold when we started to pray and after commanding out the evil spirits and releasing healing in Jesus' name, her hands started to change color from dark purple to light blue. When we finished praying, her hands were almost pink and warm to the touch. Jesus healed her circulation while we watched as the color of her hands changed right before our eyes and warmth came back into her hands. We both wept with joy. She was freed and released from the torment of infirmity by repenting, forgiving, and by the releasing of the Kingdom of God for healing and the casting out of demons. Jesus is Lord! Glory to God!

In cleansing the vessel, God calls each and every one of us to stop what we are doing in sin and turn in the opposite direction away from sin and move towards God in our thinking and actions. Jesus said in Mark 1:15 (NKJV):

The time is fulfilled, and the kingdom of God is at hand. Repent, and believe in the gospel.

Also, the apostle Peter said in Acts 2:38 (NKJV):

Then Peter said to them, "Repent, and let every one of you be baptized in the name of Jesus Christ for the remission of sins; and you shall receive the gift of the Holy Spirit.

Repent in Strong's concordance # 3340 means "reconsider morally;" also #3340 means "reversal of decision."

It actually means you used to think a sinful way but now you choose to think a moral way. Thus, your thinking changed direction and you now choose to live a moral lifestyle. By the way, the change will be evident to every one thus proving your repentance. Repentance without a changed behavior is not true repentance. There must be a moral lifestyle change turning away from sin to be true repentance.

Repentance was preached throughout the whole Bible. It is the start of cleansing our vessel. Sin did not stop when you said the sinner's prayer, No it didn't; for repentance is a continuous process of turning away from sin.

In many instances it means changing your friends. When I was in the world, my friends were of the world. After conversion I did not hang out with them, but when I did encounter them, I testified about the saving grace of Jesus to them. They didn't remain my friends after they heard my testimonies.

2 Corinthians 6:17-18 (NKJV)

> *Therefore Come out from among them and be separate, says the Lord.*
> *Do not touch what is unclean, and I will receive you. I will be a Father to you, And you shall be My sons and daughters, Says the LORD Almighty.*

The Bible also tells us to cleanse ourselves in 2 Corinthians 7:1 (NKJV):

> *Therefore, having these promises, beloved, let us cleanse ourselves from all filthiness of the flesh and spirit, perfecting holiness in the fear of God.*

Family, God will not do the separating or the cleansing for us. We are responsible to do it ourselves. I want you to notice that Paul included himself by saying **cleanse ourselves.** Paul was just like you and me. He was in a continuous struggle against the demonic realm, which will gladly lead us into sin. That is probably why he wrote in Philippians 3:12-15:

> *Not that I have already attained, or am already perfected; but I press on, that I may lay hold of that for which Christ Jesus has also laid hold of me. Brethren, I do not count myself to have apprehended; but one thing I do, forgetting those things which are behind and reaching forward to those things which are ahead, I press toward the goal for the prize of the upward call of God in Christ Jesus. Therefore let us, as many as are*

mature, have this mind;

Paul's example of cleansing ourselves should be our example.

1. Acknowledge our need for cleansing.

2. Reach out to God for it.

3. Press on to obtain it.

Paul, God bless him, did not live behind a religious front. Many are hindered in their effort to cleanse themselves, because they are not honest about themselves. It grieves the Holy Spirit when people say to themselves and others that they don't have issues or problems when indeed they do. Another way of cleansing is the casting out of evil spirits (demons) as in Matthew 12:28 (NKJV)

But if I cast out demons by the Spirit of God, surely the kingdom of God has come upon you.

Jesus depended on the Spirit of God, the Holy Spirit for discernment, direction, and power. In the process of cleansing, we too must depend on the Holy Spirit for these things.

Now we will start the process of cleansing by the casting out of demons that have attached themselves to our minds and flesh. Demons leave in the name of Jesus.

Pray with me.

Lord, I have been a sinner and my generational line has sinned also. There are transgressions and iniquity. I ask that you forgive my ancestors and myself for all our sins. I believe Jesus died on the cross for me and my ancestors. I accept and receive the blood that you shed on the cross for me and my family. I accept You as my personal Savior. You died and rose from the dead for me. I apply the shed blood of Jesus to the curses that have followed me throughout my generational line and declare that the blood of Jesus has set me free from all my sins and all curses. Jesus became the curse for me and was nailed to

the tree (Gal. 3:13) And now I command every demon and curses assigned to my family generational bloodline to drop off their assignment and be void of power over me. The shed blood of Jesus is for my salvation, healing and deliverance from demons.

Father, forgive me for holding unforgiveness toward people who have offended me and to those who I have offended, please send a spirit of forgiveness to them.

As the Holy Spirit is revealing the faces or names of those that come to your mind start forgiving. Say, "I release (name the people) and I forgive them now in Jesus' name."

As a believer in Jesus Christ, I take the authority that Jesus gave me when he said in Luke 10:19 (NKJV):

"*Behold, I give you the authority to trample on serpents and scorpions, and over all the power of the enemy, and nothing shall by any means hurt you."*

I also apply the scripture that Jesus said in Matthew 18:18 (NKJV):

"Assuredly, I say to you, whatever you bind on earth will be bound in heaven, and whatever you loose on earth will be loosed in heaven".

I, therefore, with the authority given to me by Jesus Christ, and the power of the Holy Spirit, take the authority over and bind every evil spirit that has enticed me, harassed me, compelled me, enslaved me, caused me addictions, defiled me, deceived me, attacked my physical body, or attacked my soul and tormented me, and I command them to be bound and powerless in Jesus' name

Next, we are going to cast out all unclean, evil, demonic spirits that have afflicted you, harassed you, and influenced you. They come out in the name of Jesus and they come out in the breath. When Jesus cast them out, they came out in a loud voice. There is a lot of breath that is expelled in order to make a loud voice. An interesting thing is that in the "Vines Complete Expository Dictionary" the Greek word for spirit and breath is the same word. ("pneuma"). When Jesus was casting out evil spirits they came out on a loud voice. (Mark1:26) It takes a lot of breath (pneuma) a lot of "pneuma was expelled, that is breath/spirit. So in this deliverance, as an act of your will, I will ask you to blow out breath in the name of Jesus to start the process of (evil) "spirits" leaving. They don't come out because you blow breath (pnuema), but they come out in the name of Jesus.

I command out of me every evil spirit of resentment, bitterness, hatred, distrust, unforgiveness, violence, temper, anger, murder; I command these demons and all kindred demons, to leave me now in Jesus' name. Now take a breath and blow out breath. Go! Come out of me in the name of Jesus.

I command out of me all self-willed spirits, rebellion, stubbornness, disobedience, anti-submissiveness, egotism. In the name of Jesus Christ, come out of me. Now take a breath and blow out breath. Go! Come out of me in the name of Jesus.

I command out of me all spirits of contention, strife, bickering, argument, quarreling, fighting, criticism. I command these demons and all kindred demons, to leave me now in Jesus' name. Now take a breath and blow out breath, Go in the name of Jesus.

I command out of me every spirit of control, possessiveness, dominance, witchcraft, Jezebel, Mamma's boy, dictatorial, every spirit that would cause me to place someone under my thumb to rule them. I command those spirits of control and all kindred spirits to leave me now in Jesus' name. Now take a breath and blow out breath. Go! Come out of me in the name of Jesus.

I command out of me every spirit that says, I'm going to get even, every spirit of revenge, retaliation, destruction, spite, hatred, sadism, hurt, cruelty, mutilation. I command these demons and all kindred demons, to leave me now in Jesus' name. Now take a breath and blow out breath. Go! Come out of me in the name of Jesus.

I command out of me every spirit of accusation, judging, criticism, fault finding, doctrinal error, when I listened to another gospel, and followed another Jesus, false teachings. Now take a breath and blow out breath. Come out of me in the name of Jesus.

Now repeat after me. "Jesus gave me authority and power over all the power of the enemy (Luke 10:19) therefore, I command the power of this illness, syndrome, infirmity, sickness to be void of its power over me and I break it off of my life and flesh in the name of Jesus Christ. I apply the shed blood of Jesus to these illnesses. By His stripes, I am healed. (Isaiah 53:5 and 1 Peter 2:24)."

I command out of me every demon that **attacks my physical body** with sickness, disease, or infirmities – now you name your disease, your sickness, your syndrome, your illness. Describe them by what they do or the name or title that the doctor gave it. Do this out loud.

Speak the name of the infirmity and illness and say to it, " You, the spirit of (now name it) Come out of me in the name of Jesus." Now take a breath and blow out breath. Go, in the name of Jesus.

I command out of me every demon that **defiles** me to come out of me in Jesus' name. Lustful thoughts, imaginations, impure thoughts, fantasies, I command out and away from me every evil spirit that **entices** me. Lord Jesus, you teach us to pray in Matt. 6:13 "And do not lead us into temptation, but deliver us from the evil one." I therefore command every enticing spirit that tempts me to do evil to leave me in Jesus' name. Now take a breath and blow out breath. Go, in the name of Jesus.

I command every **harassing** spirit that engineers situations in my life so that I will stumble, every spirit that sets me up for a fall, to go in Jesus' name. Now take a breath and blow out breath. Go, in the name of Jesus.

I command out of me every demon that **compels me in any way:** Obsessive compulsive behavior, excessive cleaning, excessive hand washing, excessive counting, excessive checking and rechecking, to leave me now in Jesus' name.

I command out of me every spirit that causes

addictions: alcohol, caffeine, the chase, chronic illness, compulsive lying, obsessed with church, prescription medication, drugs (illegal), emotional abuse, physical abuse, pain, over-eating, nicotine, money, female dependency, male dependency, love (obsessive), gambling, fighting, sexual abuse, sexual addictions, obsession with shopping, credit cards, Soap Operas, sugar, obsessive talking, telephone, television, video games, work and any other thing I am addicted to, name your addiction. I command those demons to leave me now in Jesus' name. Now take a breath and blow out breath. Go, in the name of Jesus.

I command out of me every demon that **enslaves** me to spirits of perversion, fornication, adulteries, homosexuality, lesbianism, prostitution, masturbation, or any demon that enslaves me, any compulsive behavior. I command those demons to leave me now in Jesus' name. Now take a breath and blow out breath. Go, in the name of Jesus.

I command out of me every demon that **tortures** and **torments** me. Lord, you heard me when I asked you to forgive me for holding a grudge when I held unforgiveness toward another. You heard me when I released them from my heart. And now I command all spirits that were assigned to **torture** me, to drop their assignments and leave me in Jesus' name.

All spirits of: unforgiveness, bitterness, resentfulness, hatred, jealousy, retaliation, and kindred spirits of loneliness, depression, despair, despondency, defeat, hopelessness, heaviness, disgust, gloom, death, suicide, death wish, insanity, senility, bipolar, mental disorder, confusion, mind binding spirits, double mindedness, schizophrenia, false front, false personalities, madness, fear of people, fear of germs, paranoia, hallucinations, all evil spirits of the mind, the spirit of Magor-Missabib (fear all around me – Jer. 20:3), dread, anxiety, compulsive and persistent fear, and the spirit that causes me fear of a mental disorder, I command those demons to leave me now in Jesus' name. Now take a breath and blow out

breath. Go, in the name of Jesus.

I command out of me every demon that has caused me to dry up spiritually, that is occupying me when I should be occupying the land. I command every spirit that dried me up, to leave me now in Jesus' name. Now take a breath and blow out breath. Go, in the name of Jesus.

I command out of me all **deceiving** spirits. In the name of Jesus, I command out of me every spirit of **deception**, self deception, lying spirits, spirits that cause me to lie, spirits that lie to me, spirits of frustration, spirits that cause religious error, every spirit of defeatism, witchcraft, unbelief, doubt, skepticism, uncontrollable anger, anti-Christ, anti- anointing, devil worship, divination, false gifting, occultism, fear that deceives, spirits of error, confusion, self deception, lying, contention, finger pointing, accusation, rebellion, strife, rejection, spiritual blindness, spiritual deafness, doctrinal error, hyper spirituality, hyper sensitivity, spirits that mix the holy with the profane, all perverse spirits, spirits of the New Age, spirits that maintain a form of godliness but deny the power thereof.

I command them to leave me now in the name of Jesus. Now take a breath and blow out breath. Go, in the name of Jesus.

In the name of Jesus, I command out of me all spirits of hypocrisy, deceit, flattery, paranoia, irritability, irrationality, pride, haughtiness, apprehension, agitation, dullness of comprehension, spirits that hinder the hearing of sermons, spirits that hinder the hearing of the Word, spirits that block faith principles, spirits of false doctrine, false prophecy, spirits that twist the scriptures, twist the truth, spirits that cause me to be defensive all the time, contention, mental confusion, spirits that hinder prayer, that hinder the move of the Holy Spirit, unsubmissive spirits that pull me away from God and from godly people, spirits that cause me to be unteachable, argumentative, fearful, spirits that cause me to blurt out my thought without thinking, impatience, spirits of control, suppressed anger, rage, resentment, unforgiveness, hate, self hate, bitterness, root of bitterness, spirits that cause me to wander from the truth, deception, chronic dissatisfaction, mind binding, incoherence, forgetfulness, delusion, self delusion.

I command them to leave me now in the name of Jesus. Now take a breath and blow out breath. Go, in the name of Jesus.

I command out of me every spirit that has deceived me, every spirit of deception, insecurity, inferiority, loneliness, self pity, timidity, shyness, ineptness, jealousy, rejection, the spirit that says, "I'm unacceptable, I'll never amount to anything, I'll never be any good, every spirit that lies to me and says I am unloved, unwanted, cast aside, out cast," Now take a breath and blow out breath. Go, in the name of Jesus.

Let me stop the deliverance here and pray for your healing. Rejection is one of the biggest problems in the church. Sometimes rejection can come to us at an early age even when we are being formed in the womb. One of the parents may have said, "I don't want this child," and in the womb you might have received the spirit of those words and rejection entered you. Place your hands over your heart and these words aloud:

Lord, I command the spirit of rejection out of me that entered me when people rejected me, when friends rejected me, when my parents rejected me, when my teachers rejected me, when society rejected me. I command this rejection to leave me now in Jesus' name. Now take a breath and blow out breath. Go, in the name of Jesus.

I now ask the Holy Spirit to come and take the place of all these evil spirits I just cast out. Jesus I give all these areas of my life to You to rule and reign in.

Keep your hands over your heart and pray for the healing of your heart.

Dear Lord, I receive acceptance from you, Lord. You are my Father and I know that you love and accept me. Heart, be healed of the wound of rejection in Jesus' name.

Chapter 2
How Do You Know if You Need Deliverance

"For we do not wrestle against flesh and blood, but against principalities, against powers, against the rulers of the darkness of this age, against spiritual hosts of wickedness in the heavenly places". Ephesians 6:12

Family, the Word of God says that we are at war with forces we cannot see with the naked eye. These forces are spiritual in nature. It is my desire in this book to expose these spiritual forces that work against our lives and to cast them out and off of our lives. Next, I would like to give you a quick overview of what the ministry of Jesus is truly about.

Jesus Christ is the same yesterday, today, and forever. (Hebrews 13:8 (NKJV). And because He never changes, His ministries never change. The four ministries of Jesus Christ were and still are:

1. The Gospel (preaching the Word of the Kingdom of God)

2. Miracles

3. Healing

4. Casting out of demons

For this purpose the Son of God was manifested, that He might destroy the works of the devil. 1 John 3:8 (NKJV)

A good portion of Jesus' ministry was the casting out of demons. The evidence of the gospel of the kingdom of God are the miracles, healing, and casting out of demons.

But if I cast out demons with the finger of God, surely

the kingdom of God has come upon you. Luke 11:20 (NKJV) also stated in *Matthew* 12:28 (NKJV): *But if I cast out demons by the Spirit of God, surely the kingdom of God has come upon you.*

So, Jesus is saying that deliverance is by the Spirit of God, by the finger of God coming to bring the Kingdom of God upon people. He also tells us in Matthew 12, that demons are cast out by the Spirit of God.

Do you see it family? Deliverance from demons is when a person, empowered by the Holy Spirit, allows himself to be the finger of God, to bring the Kingdom of God upon a person or a situation by casting out demons.

One of the first things Jesus did after he was baptized and came out of the wilderness was to gather a few disciples and go into the temple (church) to teach.

> *Now there was a man in their synagogue with an unclean spirit. And he cried out, saying, "Let us alone! What have we to do with You, Jesus of Nazareth? Did You come to destroy us? I know who You are—the Holy One of God!"*
>
> *But Jesus rebuked him, saying, "Be quiet, and come out of him!" And when the unclean spirit had convulsed him and cried out with a loud voice, he came out of him. Then they were all amazed, so that they questioned among themselves, saying, "What is this? What new doctrine is this? For with authority He commands even the unclean spirits, and they obey Him."* Mark 1:23-27 (NKJV)

One of the instructions of Jesus for believers is to cast out demons. He instructed them before his resurrection in Matthew 10:7-8 (NKJV)

> *And as you go, preach, saying, 'The kingdom of heaven is at hand.' Heal the sick, cleanse the lepers, raise the dead, cast out demons. Freely you have received, freely give.*

And after His resurrection in Mark 16:15-18 (NKJV): *And He said to them, "Go into all the world and preach the gospel to every creature. He who believes and is baptized will be saved; but he who does not believe will be condemned. And these signs will follow those who believe: In My name they will cast out demons; they will speak with new tongues; they will take up serpents; and if they drink anything deadly, it will by no means hurt them; they will lay hands on the sick, and they will recover."*

Family, one of the signs of a believer, according to Jesus, is that they will cast out demons. And by the way, did you happen to see the location of this verse, when He spoke this? It is at the very end of the book of Mark. Mark records these as some of the last words Jesus spoke on this earth before He was taken up in the cloud. He was driving the point home that this is what His followers were supposed to look and act like. He called us to do what He did on earth.

Most assuredly, I say to you, he who believes in Me, the works that I do he will do also; and greater works than these he will do, because I go to My Father. John 14:12 (NKJV)

How do you know if you need Deliverance?

Well, first of all, most of our problems are of a carnal nature. Ninety-five percent of our spiritual problems originate in our souls. We do what we do because we want to do what we do and we don't want to give up what we do, because we just want to do it. We can't cast out flesh can we? No, but it would simplify things if we could. What do you have to do with flesh? Crucify it. It has to die. You have to die to sin as Paul tells us in Roman 6:6 (NKJV):

"knowing this, that our old man was crucified with Him, that the body of sin might be done away with, that we should no longer be slaves of sin. For he who has died has been freed from sin. Now if we died with Christ, we

*believe that we shall also live with Him, knowing that Christ, having been raised from the dead, dies no more. Death no longer has dominion over Him. For the death that He died, He died to sin once for all; but the life that He lives, He lives to God. Likewise you also**, reckon yourselves to be dead indeed to sin, but alive to God in Christ Jesus our Lord**. Therefore do not let sin reign in your mortal body, that you should obey it in its lusts".*

Paul tells how to die to sin in Romans 12:1-2 (NKJV)

"I beseech you therefore, brethren, by the mercies of God, that you present your bodies a living sacrifice, holy, acceptable to God, which is your reasonable service. And do not be conformed to this world, but be transformed by the renewing of your mind, that you may prove what is that good and acceptable and perfect will of God".

Basically the Word is telling us that we have to lay our life down. (what we think is important) as a sacrifice to God, and change the way we think to what is **good** and **acceptable** to the will of God. Thought patterns have to change from worldly to Godly. Paul paints a broader picture of what is the renewing of our mind.

"...that you put off, concerning your former conduct, the old man which grows corrupt according to the deceitful lusts, *and be renewed in the spirit of your mind, and that you put on the new man which was created according to God, in true righteousness and holiness".* Ephesians 4:22-24 (NKJV)

Let's look at this a little more carefully. The old nature or the flesh is filled or corrupted with deceitful lust. Deceit means: misrepresentation, falsehood, intentional fraud, betrayal, double- dealing, trickery, insincerity, to mislead or cheat.

The old nature, the non-crucified flesh, **lust** after these things. It is when we **crucify** these things that the mind can be renewed in the likeness of God in true righteousness and holiness.

So, if you have a problem and you have done all this, that is, crucifying the flesh and you have fasted and prayed and the problem doesn't seem to go away, then we can look at the problem as being of demonic influence or some demons that are connected with that problem. Now, there are several ways of knowing if somebody needs deliverance.

First of all, by discerning of spirits.

Notice that I said discerning of spirits. It is discernment, not suspicion or formulas; it is not guess work. A lot of people operate in suspicion and believe they have a gift. Family, discerning of spirits is when the Holy Spirit discloses to you the source of theproblem as you are ministering to others.

When ministering to people, I just listen to the Holy Spirit as they speak and hear what the Holy Spirit places in my mind, because I have prayed that the Holy Spirit will reveal the source of the spiritual problem and quicken the gifts that He has given to me. So I just listen and when I have heard, I speak it. Because I have prayed, He directs my pathway. That is what you must do, pray: "You are my God, my Lord and my Savior. I acknowledge You. Please quicken the gift of the Holy Spirit," – and He will do it family! Amen!

Some people see the demonic spirits with their eyes or in their mind; others get a word of knowledge or an impression or vision from the Holy Spirit. Many times I pray for people and get an impression, a word, or vision from the Holy Spirit.

One time a woman with the aid of a walker came to me for prayers and asked me to pray for her knees. She was suffering with pain. As I laid my hands on her to pray, the Holy Spirit told me to take my hands off of her and He gave me a vision of the face of another woman and a word of knowledge "unforgiveness" I told the woman that she had unforgiveness towards a woman and she knew who it was I was speaking about. She screamed and said it was her daughter who stole her house from her. **I told the lady that because of her unforgiveness, God has sent her to the tormentors (Matt. 18:34-35), and the only way to be healed is to forgive her daughter.** She sat there crying for awhile and then she said O.K. I will forgive her and she made a public confession of her sin and asked God to forgive her of holding a grudge. After that I laid my hands on her and cast out the spirits of unforgiveness, grudge holding, hate, bitterness and like spirits. After she was set free, I prayed for her healing and instantly she jumped up and started leaping and dancing praising the Lord for God healed her instantly.

Discerning of spirits works with a word of knowledge or impressions, or visions.

Some may ask, what is a word of knowledge? It is knowledge that only God knows and then He reveals it to you, and when that word is declared and spoken, it reveals what was hidden in the dark and brings it into the light. It brings healing and deliverance. These are some of the ways the gifts of the Holy Spirit operates.

Another way you know when deliverance is necessary is by the symptoms.

When you go to a doctor, you start by describing all your symptoms and then he starts to practice on you. He has learned a lot from his medical training so he says, let's try this to see if this will clear it up. It cleared up about 90 out of 100 patients before you. It doesn't clear up, so you go back and he tries another proven remedy and that works. But we don't have to give educated guesses, because the Holy Spirit knows what the source of the problem is and He reveals it to us. I usually ask what the symptoms are first so I will have a road map to the source of the problem. I pray deliverance for saved and unsaved alike. I have seen people who were not saved become saved because a demon was cast out of them. Then they retain their deliverance when they have the knowledge of Christ and are walking with Jesus. An unsaved person does not have the fundamental knowledge of Christ and it is harder for them to hold their deliverance because they fall back into sin.

In Frank Marzullo Senior's book *"Eight Keys to Spiritual and Physical Health,"* he starts out by analyzing the problem. **Is it demonic, is it the flesh, or is it the human spirit? Is the person connected to the body of Christ? Do they read the Bible? Are they desperate to be healed and delivered?** I usually sit the person down and ask them to tell me about their life. If I can't see the person because of time, I have them write me an email or set up a phone conference. I prefer writing or an email for the simple reason that I have more time to pray over what I just read and ask the Lord to highlight what spirits are in operation in that person's life.

Another way to discern spirits is if there is an obvious mental disorder.

If there is confusion or irrationality. These things indicate the presence of demons. The devil wants to control your mind. That is why Paul writes in 2 Cor. 10:5 ***"to take every thought captive to the obedience of Christ."***

Family, we really have to fight irrational thoughts and command them out of our minds in Jesus' name. Why? Because there are demonic influences at the source of these problems.

One way to fight these thoughts is to ask yourself why these thoughts came into your mind, that is to say, what brought that thought into my mind? You have to ask that question when bringing deliverance either to yourself or to others. You have to ask, what is the source of that thought?

Why does that person want to die? Why does that person hate? Why do they want to drink or smoke? So you must follow the thought pattern back to the source in order to find the root cause. When you have been delivered, don't entertain the demons in your mind again.

> *"The thief does not come except to steal, and to kill, and to destroy. I have come that they may have life, and that they may have it more abundantly."* (John 10:10 NKJV)

The devil wants you sick, destroyed or dead, but God want you to have an abundant Spirit filled life; healed, delivered and full of life. Amen

By their conversation

Another way you know when someone needs deliverance is by **their conversation**. Family, you can tell what kind of a tree it is by the fruit it is producing; by their speech, by what they say, if they are lying, cursing, telling dirty stories, filthy speech, always gossiping, bragging, complaining, criticizing, judging everyone, taking offense easily and much more**.**

Family, whatever darkness that is in you will eventually come out of your mouth. Demons like to show off in their host. Many times the darkness in a person will be exposed by the attitudes of the one hosting it.

The way I find those demons is by asking a simple question such as, "Lord, what motivated that person to speak that?" The answer that the Holy Spirit brings to my mind is usually the source of the demonic problem that lies inside that person. If a person really wants to know the truth about himself, he could ask his friends if they see any faults in his speech or attitudes. Proverbs 27:6 says: *"Faithful are the wounds of a friend, But the kisses of an enemy are deceitful."* (NKJV)

Another way that you know when someone needs

deliverance is when they are having problem in the sexual realm.

Unclean sexual acts, perversions, sexual fantasies – If someone is fascinated with pornography, you already know the source of the problem, it is lust. Some with sexual problems dress provocatively. Demons like to draw attention to themselves, they like to brag and show off. Extra tight clothing that clings to the form of the body, women showing more cleavage than they should, men exposing their chest, wearing tight pants. Spirits of lust motivates this and spirits of control could also be behind this, but it may be rooted in rejection.

Addiction Problems

Also, you know you need deliverance when there is addiction to certain substances such as: tobacco, alcohol, drugs, caffeine, coca cola, tea, sugar, sweets. How do you know that you need deliverance from these things? Well, if you have done everything that you can, everything that is possible to break the habits, you have resisted, fasted, prayed, and nothing works, well then you might need deliverance not only from the demon that produced that particular problem, but deliverance from addiction itself. If you leave the main spirit of addiction, it will be a bridge to another demonic problem if you don't deal with the root of addiction.

Another realm in which deliverance is necessary is when there are infirmities:

"And behold, there was a woman who had a spirit of infirmity eighteen years, and was bent over and could in no way raise herself up. But when Jesus saw her, He called her to Him and said to her, "Woman, you are loosed from your infirmity." And He laid His hands on her, and immediately she was made straight, and glorified God." Luke 13:11-13 (NKJV)

The evil spirit of infirmity had to be cast out first, and

then the laying on of hands for healing. I follow this example when I pray for healing. I cast out the evil spirit that is in control of the illness, sickness, or disease, infirmity and then I lay hands on for healing in Jesus' name.

Example: Deaf and dumb spirits for ears and speech; for foot and leg problems, call out the spirits that cause lameness or crippling and so forth. If someone has cancer, call out the spirit cancer, spirit of division, spirit of cell sickness and separation, You, the one who divides the cell, who consumes the flesh, (call out the spirit by what it does to the person). After it is cast out, pray for healing in Jesus' name.

Deliverance is necessary when there is involvement in the realm of the occult

"Therefore evil shall come upon you; You shall not know from where it arises. And trouble shall fall upon you; You will not be able to put it off. And desolation shall come upon you suddenly, which you shall not know.

"Stand now with your enchantments and the multitude of your sorceries, in which you have labored from your youth— Perhaps you will be able to profit, Perhaps you will prevail. You are wearied in the multitude of your counsels; Let now the astrologers, the stargazers, and the monthly prognosticators stand up and save you from what shall come upon you. Behold, they shall be as stubble, the fire shall burn them; They shall not deliver themselves from the power of the flame; It shall not be a coal to be warmed by, nor a fire to sit before! Thus shall they be to you with whom you have labored, your merchants from your youth; They shall wander each one to his quarter. No one shall save you". Isaiah 47:11-15 (NKJV)

The reading of horoscopes and following occultism is an abomination to the Lord.

"When you come into the land which the LORD your God is giving you, you shall not learn to follow the abominations of those nations. There shall not be found among you anyone who makes his son or his daughter pass through the fire, or one who practices witchcraft, or a soothsayer, or one who interprets omens, or a sorcerer, or one who conjures spells, or a medium, or a spiritist, or one who calls up the dead.

For all who do these things are an abomination to the LORD, and because of these abominations the LORD your God drives them out from before you. You shall be blameless before the LORD your God. For these nations which you will dispossess listened to soothsayers and diviners; but as for you, the LORD your God has not appointed such for you." Deut. 18:9-14 (NKJV)

There are many different type of occult practices such as channeling, divination, zodiac astrology, horoscope, hypnotism, spiritism, spiritualism, Chinese astrology, numerology, tarot cards, Taoism, I Ching, Kabbalah, Zen eastern practices and religions, Buddhism, Hinduism, Vedanta, Brahmanism, Reiki, astral projection, automatic writing, runes, Ouija board, telepathy, readings from psychics, drugs, acupuncture, Mayan philosophy, fairy tales, reincarnation, karma, four leaf clover superstition, spells, fortune cookie superstition, spiritual healers, transcendental meditation, yoga, chakra, third eye, E.S.P., Ramtha cult, channeling the gods of this world, worshiping Roman, Greek, Egyptian gods , psychic powers, black magic, white magic, necromancy, soul travel, Crystal Powers, parapsychology, magic healings, demon worship, Satan worship, Lucifer worship.

If you got involved with any of these or others like them,

then you have entered Satan's kingdom through occult practices.

Involvement in a cult can open the door to demons. A cult is any religion or organization that does not believe that the only way to our heavenly Father is through the atoning shed blood of Jesus Christ, such as: Jehovah Witness, Christian Science, Unity, Theosophy, Mormonism, Freemasons, Eastern Star, Hare Krishna.

This was just a partial list, but If you have ever been involved in any occult practice, you must ask God to forgive you for it is sin and **renounce it**, then you must also **cast out** the *spirit of it* in the name of Jesus and the *spirit of the covenant* you made with the devil when you walked in agreement with him when you practiced these things.

"For if he who comes preaches another Jesus whom we have not preached, or if you receive a different spirit which you have not received, or a different gospel which you have not accepted—you may well put up with it!" 2 Corinthians 11:4 (NKJV)

You see family, when we go to any other source for spiritual power, wisdom, or knowledge besides our Heavenly Father through Jesus Christ, then we have made God jealous, for it is spiritual adultery when we have sought out another god to seek such things. Not only that, but when we go to any other spiritual source for power, wisdom, or knowledge, we open ourselves to the spirit of another Jesus and another gospel. After a person repents, those spirits must be cast out. Renouncing and casting out are two different things.

Another way to know if deliverance is needed is with your natural eye.

Sometimes demons manifest in the expressions of the ones they inhabit. Sometime I will be praying for a person and the demons in that person will start making them roll their eyes back in the sockets, so all you see is the white of their eyes, or a twitching nose or their hands and feet that claw-up. This usually indicates the presence of occult or witchcraft spirits.

If someone closes their eyes hard and tight so they won't have to look at the one ministering to them, or rigid fingers This usually indicates lust of the eyes, pornography or masturbation. 1 John 2:16 says:

> *For all that is in the world—the **lust of the flesh**, the **lust of the eyes**, and the **pride of life**—is not of the Father but is of the world.* (NKJV)

I would classify those as 3 main demonic forces that afflict mankind; spirits of **lust of the flesh, lust of the eyes** and **pride.**

Another spirit that you can see in the natural is a **mocking spirit**. All spirits mock, but there is a difference with the one who mocks the minister. It does so defiantly. It usually is accompanied by facial expressions of smirks and laughing.

Sometimes people have **pains in their reproductive organs**.
This usually has to do with occult and witchcraft spirits.

A woman came for deliverance who had an incubus spirit. What is that you might ask? They are spirits that have sex with a woman. A succubus spirit has sex with men. You will find both of those definitions in the dictionary.

She came because this incubus came to her in the form of a lizards and inserted their hands up her vagina day and night. This was driving her crazy and while I was ministering to her they started again. When dealing with incubus, it is imperative that the minister go to the source. The minister has to find what gave the incubus the right to enter a person and then through the shed blood of Jesus Christ cancel their right to torment the victim in that area. She had gotten into occultism and this gave those demons the right to harass her. Once she renounced her involvement and asked God to forgive her, I commanded those spirits out in Jesus' name and they left her. Glory to God! I saw her a few years later in the grocery store and she was still free from those spirits.

Another time I ministered to a woman who was on the verge of a divorce because an incubus in the form of a male came between her and her husband and had sex with her while her husband was trying to make love to her. This placed a strain on their marriage and was driving them both crazy. As I ministered to her, the spirit manifested and she thrashed around on the floor. Her husband sat on her legs to hold them from kicking and I called out the incubus spirit. It spoke out of her with a demonic tongue (Satan has counterfeit tongues), not the Holy Spirit tongue and cried out, "Leave us alone. We have a right to be here"

It is important to find out if they do, so I stopped the deliverance for a short prayer. I prayed "Father, reveal to me in the Holy Spirit what right this demon has to be here and when it came in." Immediately I knew in the Holy Spirit that this incubus came into her on her father's side of the family line when her great- grandfather seven generations back, made a pact with Satan and worshiped him. I called out the spirit that entered her blood line back seven generations and commanded that curse to be void of its power over her, because the blood of Jesus that was shed for her. I proclaimed that the blood of Jesus canceled the curse. As soon as I said those words, she vomited. I found out after her deliverance that she came from a long line of Santeria and Santero witchcraft.

Go to the source of entry by asking the Holy Spirit to reveal it and cancel all ungodly contracts in Jesus name. Then cast out those evil spirits.

Sometimes incubus causes a woman to be barren, because they want that womb for their own sexual desires. They kill the male seed.

Cold hands can indicate poor circulation, but sometimes it indicates a spirit of death.

A buzzing noise in the head or ears, mental disorder, confusion, mania, madness sometimes indicate occultism.

A drooling or running nose during deliverance could indicate spirits of lust or unclean sexual spirits.

SEVEN BLOCKAGES TO DELIVERANCE:

1. Unforgiveness – Matt. 18:21-35

2. Occultism, cults, and false religions (seeking other gods, or powers, knowledge or wisdom form sources other than the God of Israel through Jesus Christ)

"You shall have no other gods before Me."You shall not make for yourself a carved image—any likeness of anything that is in heaven above, or that is in the earth beneath, or that is in the water under the earth; you shall not bow down to them nor serve them. For I, the LORD your God, am a jealous God, visiting the iniquity of the fathers upon the children to the third and fourth generations of those who hate Me, but showing mercy to thousands, to those who love Me and keep My commandments. Exodus 20:3-6 (NKJV)

God is a jealous God. He is jealous for our love. He doesn't want to share us with any other gods. He sees any type of occultism, cults, or false religions as spiritual adultery.

3. Abortion. As the Baal worshipers threw their children into the fires to sacrifice to their gods, Molech and Chemosh, today's women sacrifice their unborn children on the altar of shame or inconvenience. In God's eyes, it is still throwing the baby into the fire.

4. Unconfessed sin blocks deliverance. If the spirits won't go in the name of Jesus, then they have a legal right to be there. They cling to their legal rights. Pray and ask the Lord to reveal why they have a right to stay, and he will reveal it to you. A thought will come into your mind as to what you may have done 30 years ago. Confess it as sin and it will destroy the legal right of that spirit.

5 Possessing Idols-- Ex. 20:3-6. As stated before, you can make anything an idol in your life. Your wife, your husband, your children, your job, your car, your jewelry, your wealth, statutes, pictures, CD's, etc.

6. Possession of Amulets, such as a lucky coin, brass bracelets for healing, Italian horn for warding off evil, or horoscope sign and so forth. Any time you wear or keep an amulet you invite demons of darkness to you. It doesn't ward off evil, it draws evil to you.

The Lord told Israel to destroy the idols that they came across and not to covet the gold or silver that is on them.

> *You shall burn the carved images of their gods with fire; you shall not covet the silver or gold that is on them, nor take it for yourselves, lest you be snared by it; for it is an abomination to the LORD your God. Nor shall you bring an abomination into your house, lest you be doomed to destruction like it. You shall utterly detest it and utterly abhor it, for it is an accursed thing.* Deuteronomy 7:25-26 (NKJV)

We have a fire pit in our back yard where people bring XXX movies, books on the New Age, pictures, letters, charms, scarab beetles and gods of every kind, and we burn them up, singing worship songs to the Lord Jesus Christ. Anytime you place your trust in powers or knowledge, from any other source than God the Father through Jesus Christ, you are bowing to a graven image.

7. Pride, embarrassment, or comfort in their affliction will block you from receiving deliverance.

Sometimes people will just sit there during deliverance fighting a move of God in their lives. They don't want anyone to know that the sweet, kind person that they appear to be, has a demon. If they did find out, they would have to move out of the county, or they take pleasure in people waiting on them due to their affliction.

Those are some reasons why people stop their own deliverance. Jesus said to the man at the pool of Bethesda, in John 5:5 "Do you want to be made well? (NKJV) Some people don't wish to be healed.

Next, we are going to cast out all unclean, evil, demonic spirits that have afflicted you, harassed you, and influenced you.

PREPARATION FOR DELIVERANCE --AND REAFFIRMING OUR SALVATION-

Pray the following:

Lord, Jesus, I accept you as my Savior, my God, and my King. You died on the cross and resurrected from the dead. You saved me and redeemed me with your precious blood. I belong to you, and surrender my whole life to you from this day forward. Please forgive me of all my sins. I renounce and **separate myself from all practices of sin. I call upon you, Lord, to deliver me from the lies and deceptions of the enemy. I take the authority that was given to me by Jesus Christ when He said in Luke 10:19,** *"Behold, I give you the authority to trample on serpents and scorpions, and over all the power of the enemy, and nothing shall by any means hurt you. And also in Matthew* **18:18,** *"Assuredly, I say to you, whatever you bind on earth will be bound in heaven, and whatever you loose on earth will be loosed in heaven".* *(NKJV)*

I now command every demon that is in me or influences me or oppresses me to be bound and powerless in Jesus' name. I command them to be loosed from me now in Jesus' name.

In the name of Jesus Christ, I command out of me spirits of:

Misrepresentation, falsehood, intentional fraud, lying, theft, betrayal, double dealing, trickery, insincerity, to mislead or cheater. Sexual perversion lust, pornography, homosexual, masturbation, lesbian, fantasy lust, orgies, ritualistic sex, rape, sexual daydreaming, sexual dreams, incubus, succubus, abortions, addictions, to alcohol, sugar, tobacco, drugs, movies, sports, gambling, addiction to anything, lying, cursing, dirty stories, filthy talk, spirits that make me always be gossiping, bragging, complaining, criticizing, judging everyone, taking offense easily.

Leave me in Jesus' name. Now take a deep breath and blow it out. Go in Jesus' name.

In the name of Jesus Christ, I command out of me spirits of:

Mental Disorders – disorders that are persistent and ever present that cause:

confusion, irrationality clouded mind, insanity, madness, crazy thinking, Schizophrenia, double-mindedness, indecision, forgetfulness, indifference, apathy, mental breakdown, multiple personality, vivid imagination, daydreaming, unreality, fantasy, poor judgment, poor thinking, lethargy, depression, death wish, suicide, guilt, embarrassment, shame, mind-binding spirits, bipolar, false personalities, senility, fear of people, fear of germs, paranoia, hallucinations, all evil spirits of the mind, octopus spirits, twisted thinking, always looking for something wrong, negativity, false compassion, inordinate affection for animals, suspicion, distrust, always feeling under persecution.

Leave me in Jesus' name. Now take a deep breath and blow it out. Go in Jesus' name.

Lord, I confess that I held unforgiveness in my heart towards………..(Name them).

I command out of me the spirits of :

Unforgiveness, resentment, hate, bitterness, root of bitterness, envy, jealousy, retaliation, revenge, self-resentment and pride, doubt, unbelief, skepticism, worry, anger, rage, temper, ranting and raving, violence, murder.

Now take a deep breath and blow it out. Go in Jesus' name.

In the name of Jesus, I command out of me the spirits of:

Occultism... idolatry, Ouija board, palmistry, handwriting analysis, automatic handwriting, E.S.P., hypnotism, horoscope (including the name of your zodiac sign), fortune telling, divination, water witching, sorcery, witchcraft, vampirism-the drinking of human blood, spirit of Lilith (queen of Satan), all spirits that entered on ungodly blood covenants, (blood brothers, sisters), black magic, white magic, conjuration, incantation, charms, fetishes, Santeria, unholy impartation, curses, vexes, spells, jinxes, channeling, divination, zodiac astrology, horoscope, hypnotism, spiritism, spiritualism, Chinese astrology, numerology, tarot cards, Taoism, I Ching, Kabbalah, Zen Buddhism, Buddhism, Hinduism, vendetta, Brahmanism, Reiki, astral projection, runes, telepathy, readings from psychics, drugs, acupuncture, Mayan philosophy, fairy tales, reincarnation, karma, four leaf clover superstition, fortune cookie superstition, spiritual healers, transcendental meditation, yoga, chakras, third eye, Ramtha, channeling the gods of this world, psychic powers, necromancy, soul travel, crystal powers, parapsychology, magic healings, demon worship, Satan worship, Lucifer worship. yoga spirit of Kundulini–Hindu god, (serpent spirit coiled at the base of the spine), Transcendental Meditation, mantra, soul projection, astral-projection, idolatry in any form, spirits of other gods. Name what you got involved in.

Now take a deep breath and blow it out. Go in Jesus' name.

In the name of Jesus, I command out of me the spirits of:

Cults... Jehovah Witnesses, Christian Science, Scientology, Unity, Theosophy, Mormonism, Unification Church/Moonies, Masonic Order, Eastern Star, Hare Krishna, New Age Movement, and any other that does not believe that the only way to the Father is through the shed Blood of Jesus Christ.

Now take a deep breath and blow it out. Go in Jesus' name.

In the name of Jesus, I command out of me the spirits of:

Fear... Fear and worry of all kinds as earlier stated: Spirit of Magor-Missabib (Jer. 20:3) dread, anxiety, phobias, compulsive and persistent fear, fear of cats, dogs, fear of animals, high places, low places (depths), open places, fear of men, of women, fear being alone, fear of self, thunderstorms, crowds, blood, mice, dead bodies, fear of night, darkness, fear of reptiles, noise, fire, fear of elevators, fear of being closed in, fear of being buried alive, fear of death, fear of what may happen in the future, fear of what is thought of you, fear of what is said of you, fear of not being accepted, fear of reprisal, fear of retaliation, fear of the devil, fear of demons, fear that something is after you, fear of shadows, fear of the unknown.

Now take a deep breath and blow it out. Go in Jesus' name.

Now proclaim:

> *I sought the LORD, and He heard me and delivered me from all my fears.* **Ps. 34:4 (NKJV)**

> *For God has not given us a spirit of fear, but of power and of love and of a sound mind.* **2 Tim. 1:7 (NKJV)**

In Jesus' name I command out of me the spirits of:

Rejection, self rejection, fear of rejection, spirits that make me feel unloved, unwanted, unneeded, insecurity, inferiority, abused, tension, stress, defensiveness, judgmentalism, criticism, blame shifting, distrust, disrespect, hardness, perfectionism, withdrawal, spirits that block communication, friendship, and love, spirits that cause sadness, grief, sorrow, crushed ego, wounded or crushed spirit, inadequacy, self accusation, self condemnation, loneliness, depression, despair, self pity, despondency, unworthiness, discouragement, hopelessness, shame, defeat, escapism, death, suicide, and rejection at the moment of conception. Go in Jesus' Name

Now take a deep breath and blow it out. Go in Jesus' name.

Prayer for the wounded spirit

Jesus, you were there when I was conceived. You knew what happened to me then. You knew the hurt and the pain I felt then. Lord Jesus, supply me now with the love that wasn't there then and let your healing love come into me now. I thank you for healing my wounded spirit and broken heart. Now receive the love of the Lord Jesus as He heals your wounded spirit and broken heart. (*Taken from the book:* "Healing the Wounded Spirit and Broken Heart" by Frank Marzullo Sr.)

In the name of Jesus, I command out of me the spirits of:
Pride, haughtiness, self-righteousness, criticism, judgmentalism, murmuring, gossip, contention, fighting, vanity, arrogance, insolence, egotistism, bragging, mockery, self-assertion, perfection, stubbornness, anti-Christ, Jezebel, control, domination, manipulation, lust for power, dictatorial.

Now take a deep breath and blow it out. Go in Jesus' name.

In the name of Jesus, I command out of me the spirits of:

The tongue – hypocrisy, lying, cursing, blasphemy, gossip, blabbermouth, addiction, tobacco, drugs,(sorcery), alcohol, gluttony, obesity, compulsions, sharp tongue, curses I spoke on others.

Now take a deep breath and blow it out. Go in Jesus' name.

In the name of Jesus, I command out of me the spirits of:

Lust, fantasy lust, perversions, fornication, adultery, masturbation, Sodomy, incest, rape, homosexual, lesbian, anal sex, bestiality, sex with animals, sex with spirits, Incubus, Succubus, (LILITH) Vampire spirit, pornography, lust of the eyes, pride of life, lust of the world, whoredom, gigolo, womanizer, prostitution, multiple sex, orgies, abortion and Moloch, Baal, Chemosh, Milcom, the Ammorite gods of child sacrifice.

Now take a deep breath and blow it out. Go in Jesus' name.

In the name of Jesus, I command out of me:

the spirits that make me feel everything is unfair, victim spirit, withdrawal, fantasy, daydreaming, vivid imagination, unreality, pouting, timidity, self-awareness, shyness, overly-sensitivity, talkativeness.

Now take a deep breath and blow it out. Go in Jesus' name.

In the name of Jesus, I command out of me

the spirits of: nervousness, worry, tension, stress, pressure, insecurity, bed wetting, thumb sucking, fingernail biting, sleep-walking, spirits of failure, poverty, spirits that rob me of my wealth.

Now take a deep breath and blow it out. Go in Jesus' name.

In the name of Jesus, I command out of me the spirits of:

Infirmity, allergies, migraine headaches, and (Name your own sickness or diseases).

Now take a deep breath and blow it out. Go in Jesus' name.

Place your hand on the areas of pain in your body and pray aloud the following:

> **Dear Heavenly Father, I claim healing from head to toe by the power of the shed blood of Jesus Christ. Amen**

Chapter 3
Identifying Demons and Works of the Flesh

Now that you know that deliverance is necessary, let's look at how to identify demons by their work.

When you want to identify a person or get the attention of that person, you call that person by their name. Hi Susie, Hi Sam and they recognize that you are speaking to them. Names are used to identify people. When my wife (Jill) and I are in a store such as Wal-Mart and I know she is in an aisle or two over somewhere, I call out "Jill" and if she is there, she responds, "I'm here." I would get no response if I yelled out, "HEY YOU," where are you? No one would know who I was calling.

Names are used to identify. You receive a name at birth that identifies you for life. Demons also have names that identify them but more than that those names identify the work that they do to destroy lives. Now the devil and his demons do not want you to know that they are at work in and over your lives. They do not want to be exposed. They operate best in a person's life in obscurity and darkness. When light comes in and shines on them by identification, by whom and what they are, by naming them, their power is broken and their work is destroyed. If identification of the demon by name is not known, then calling it out by other means is the next best step.

Let's say Jill and I were back in Wal-Mart and she is a couple of aisles over so I call out, Hey you beautiful woman with the blond hair, red blouse and blue jean skirt, who is married to Frank Marzullo, come over here in the vitamin aisle. You see Family, you can make identification by other means.

Identifying spirits by what they do or their characteristics or how they manifest through a person's life by what they produce has the same effect on them. They now know that you have identified them and are speaking to them. Many times, it is a better form of identifying them and many times it is more effective in getting rid of them, Here is an example of your not knowing the name of an evil spirit, but you know the effects of what it does. Call it out in this descriptive way. "You, the one that travels in the blood, or "You, the one that attacks the liver, or "You, the one that causes arguments," or "You, the one that is always making me lose my job." Personify the demon by saying, "YOU, THE ONE THAT…. Then describe what it does, what it causes or produces in your life.

Blindness: "You, the one that causes loss of vision"

Deafness: "You, the one that causes loss of hearing, who has attacked the eardrum."

Dumbness: "You, the one that has attacked the speech, tongue, lips

When you expose evil spirits and identify them in this fashion, there is usually an immediate response. Sometimes in deliverance when calling them out by name, they speak out like they did to Jesus in: Luke 4:34 (NKJV)

> ...saying, "Let us alone! What have we to do with You, Jesus of Nazareth? Did You come to destroy us? I know who You are— the Holy One of God!"

This happens to me every once in a while also. On one occasion I was ministering at a church in Florida when a woman approached the altar for prayer. She was a Christian for over 20 years but she had a problem with profanity. As I started to pray for her, she started to curse at me and my wife at the top of her lungs using the foulest language you ever heard. I would call out the evil spirit of blasphemy, and the evil spirit would laugh at me and say out of her, "Wrong, guess again." I called out profanity and the evil spirit in her laughed and said, "Wrong, guess again."

This went on for some time as I called out spirits

associated with cursing, but each time the evil spirit in her would laugh at me and say "Wrong, guess again." I cut the deliverance off for she was not getting set free. I discerned that there was something causing a blockage to her deliverance. I sent her home to write out her life's history. I wanted to know who wounded her, who disappointed her, who let her down, who sinned against her.

She sent me a letter full of her past. At age 8, she was sexually abused by her step-grandfather and forced to perform oral sex on him. When he finished, he would pay her a quarter, thus making her a prostitute at age 8-14. At age 18 she left home to search out her real father. She found him in another state. He was running five houses of prostitution. She identified herself as his daughter and he took her in and raped her that night. She stayed his sex slave for a year and a half. She broke free, found Jesus as her savior and 20 years later found me.

A month later we met again while I was ministering at this church and now I was armed with her history. This time I started with identifying the demon by when it came in and what it did.

I said, "**YOU,** the one that came into her **when** men abused her. **YOU,** the one who came into her **when** her step-grandfather penetrated her mouth and throat, **YOU,** the one who came into her **when** she swallowed his sperm, **YOU,** the one who came into her **when** her father raped her and made her his sex slave, **YOU,** the one that came into her **when** men of authority abused her and raped her, **YOU,** the spirit of prostitution when she sold herself for money, **YOU,** the man-hating spirit and now **YOU,** the spirit of profanity come out of her in Jesus' name." She gagged and threw up all over the church floor and was set free.

In identifying the demons, be as specific as you can. Leave no room for error. Make sure that the demons know that you are identifying them. Notice that I said, "**You** that came in **when**…your step-grandfather… and….your father…I identified the demons by **who** they came in by and **when** they came in and **how** they came in and **what** they produced.

As a former City of Miami Beach Police Officer, I learned that there are elements to solving a crime and they are **Who, What, Where, When, Why** and **How**. Identifying demons by getting the person's history is like a spiritual road map.

This woman's main demon was not cursing or foul mouth, but that is what it caused. This woman's main demon was a hatred for men, especially men of authority. This hatred came into her from being sexually molested and abused by men in her family who were supposed to be her protectors but instead they abused her. This was a good example on how this woman's demonic behavior hid behind other demons that came into her from her past 25-30 years ago.

So you can call out demons by name and if no response switch to the other method by calling them out by what they do or how they came in or what they cause (who, what, when, where, why, how). God says in His Word that demons exist. Some Old Testament references are;

Deuteronomy 32:17 (NKJV)

They sacrificed to demons, not to God, to gods they did not know, to new gods, new arrivals that your fathers did not fear.

Psalm 106:37-38 (NKJV)

They even sacrificed their sons And their daughters to demons, and shed innocent blood, the blood of their sons and daughters, whom they sacrificed to the idols of Canaan; and the land was polluted with blood.

Leviticus 17:7 (NKJV)

They shall no more offer their sacrifices to demons, after whom they have played the harlot. This shall be a statute forever for them throughout their generations."

There are many references in the gospels of demons but the one I love the most is found in James 2:19 (NKJV)

You believe that there is one God. You do well. Even the demons believe—and tremble!

This is very interesting. It shows that demons have fear at the thought of God. Family, the demons also know who you are and if you walk in authority as a believer, they shudder also. In John 10:10 Jesus not only gives His plan for us, life and more abundant life, but he also gives us the whole plan of the enemy (steal, kill, destroy) that is theft, death and destruction.

Demons also have a plan to lure Christians away from their faith.

Now the Spirit expressly says that in latter times some will depart from the faith, giving heed to deceiving spirits and doctrines of demons 1 Tim. 4:1 (NKJV)

I am witnessing more and more Christians in today's times giving heed to deceiving spirits and doctrines of demons as they mix Christianity with some other worldly belief or teachings and these people have departed from the teachings of faith that Paul taught.

Rev. 16:14 warns us that demons will perform signs also. That is why I am leery of prophets and teachers and ministers who are only interested in drawing people to themselves.

We can see that demonic activity is in the Old Testament and according to www.biblegateway.com there are at least 48 references to demons or evil spirits in the New Testament.

Jesus spent a lot of His time ministering to people who had demonic problems. Jesus said," in: Matthew 12:25-26 (NKJV):

> *"Every kingdom divided against itself is brought to desolation, and every city or house divided against itself will not stand. If Satan casts out Satan, he is divided against himself. How then will his kingdom stand?"*

Jesus taught about the structure of the demonic kingdom, how they were united and not divided against themselves. He taught that Satan does not fight against Satan. If Jesus recognized that the satanic kingdom exists, then it does. Demons are not a myth or a fairytale. They are harmful evil spirits that want to attach themselves to people so that they can manifest their personalities through them. Again I repeat, they come to steal, kill and destroy. John 10:10 (NKJV)

The Bible also mentions the organizational structure of this satanic kingdom in Ephesians 6:12 (NKJV):

> *For we do not wrestle against flesh and blood, but against* **principalities,** *against* **powers,** *against the* **rulers of the darkness** *of this age, against* **spiritual hosts of wickedness** *in the heavenly places.*

These are different stations or ranks within the demonic realm or kingdom and each is responsible for precise attacks on the people of this earth and God's creation. These are unseen spiritual enemies using humans and environment to do their dirty work.

Satan's has titles. Here is a list of some of them taken from the concordance pg. 1800 of the NASB © 2000 Zondervan Corp.

Abbaddon Rev.9:11; **Accuser-**Ps.109:6,Rev.12:10; **Adversary**–1 Peter 5:8; **Apollyon**–Rev. 9:11; **Beelzebul**–Matt. 10:25, Mk. 3:22; **Belial**–2 Cor. 6:15; **Deceiver of the World**–Rev. 12:9; **Devil**–Mt. 4:1, John 6:70, 13:2, Eph. 4:27, 6:11, 1 Tim. 3:6-7, Heb. 2:14, 1 Pet. 5:8, Rev. 2:10, 20:2,10; **Dragon**-Rev.12:9; **Enemy**-Matt.13:28,39; **Evil One** – Matt. 13:19, 38, John 17:15, Eph. 6:16, 1 John 2:13,14, 5:18,19; **Father of Lies**–John 8:44; **God of this World**–2

Cor. 4:4; **Liar**–John 8:44; **Murderer**–John 8:44; **Prince of the Power of the Air**–Eph. 2:2; **Ruler of the demons** - Matt. 9:34, Mk. 3:22; **Ruler of this World**–John 12:31,14:30, 16:11; **Serpent of Old**–Rev. 12:9

In the book of Job. we see Satan using lighting, whirlwind and disease to afflict Job and his family. These are some of the unseen demonic forces (Eph. 6:12) behind catastrophes diseases, illness, loss, destruction, death and temptation.

One of the ways we can see and identify demons is by their activities or their works. As I pointed out in Chapter 1, quoting Derek Prince, demons entice, they harass, they compel, they enslave, they cause addictions, they defile they deceive, and they attack the physical body and they torture. When you see these things present in a person's life, know that demonic activity may be present, however not all the time. Sometimes it may be the result of the fallen nature of man or natural causes.

The Bible says in Romans 3:23 (NKJV) *"for all have sinned and fall short of the glory of God"*. Sin has defiled every living being. This fallen nature in Romans 6:6 is called *"the old man,"* and in Gal. 5:24 it is called *"the flesh."* In Rom. 8:6 it is called
"carnally minded."

Even though all people are fallen, not all people come under the power of demons. So when identifying demons and their work, it is imperative to identify if it is the fallen flesh nature or if it is demons.

The Bible speaks of the flesh in Galatians 5:16-21 (NKJV)

"I say then: Walk in the Spirit, and you shall not fulfill the lust of the flesh. For the flesh lusts against the Spirit, and the Spirit against the flesh; and these are contrary to one another, so that you do not do the things that you wish. But if you are led by the Spirit, you

are not under the law. Now the works of the flesh are evident, which are: adultery, fornication, uncleanness, lewdness, idolatry, sorcery, hatred, contentions, jealousies, outbursts of wrath, selfish ambitions, dissensions, heresies, envy, murders, drunkenness, revelries, and the like; of which I tell you beforehand, just as I also told you in time past, that those who practice such things will not inherit the kingdom of God."

Family it is the devil's objective and desire to keep you practicing the lusts of the flesh. According to the words of Jesus, if the devil can succeed in this, those who continue to indulge their flesh will not inherit the kingdom of God.

Jesus explained to us our carnal inclinations, those things that operate out of the heart of men.

For from within, out of the heart of men, proceed evil thoughts, adulteries, fornications, murders, thefts, covetousness, wickedness, deceit, lewdness, an evil eye, blasphemy, pride, foolishness. All these evil things come from within and defile a man." Mark 7:21-23 (NKJV)

Demons are drawn to the flesh and will attach themselves to assist you in continuing practicing the works of the flesh. They attach to areas of your evil desires.

Instead, we must declare and claim this scripture found in Galatians 2:20 (NKJV)

I have been crucified with Christ; it is no longer I who live, but Christ lives in me; and the life which I now live in the flesh I live by faith in the Son of God, who loved me and gave Himself for me.

But a lot of Christians never seem to live a victorious life producing the fruit of the Holy Spirit; love, joy, peace, patience, kindness, goodness, faithfulness, gentleness and self control (Gal 5:22-23) because they never learned to crucify their life in Christ. They never committed that part of the Word to their lives. To them the part that says in Galatians 5:20, "I no longer live, but Christ lives in me," surely must have been meant for someone else. That is why they struggle. They never practiced crucifying their flesh, those things that Jesus said were in us, also those things that Paul described as a manifestation of deeds of the flesh.

Crucifying the flesh, the carnal desires, is our remedy to fix our fleshly nature. Many times by living a crucified life, we avoid demonic attachments because demons attach themselves to a person who is still practicing their old sinful ways.

Family, before we start deliverance, it is important that we repent. Repentance means to turn away from our sins. I ask you to pray this prayer with me now and at this time I ask you to reflect upon your life and confess your sins that you struggle with. Bring them before the Lord in prayer.

Pray sincerely:

Lord Jesus, I have sinned and struggled with fleshly desires. I choose to turn away from temptations and I am very sorry for sinning. Please forgive me Lord. (*Now as your sins are coming before your face, repent of them and turn away from them, promising not to do them anymore. For the Lord Jesus Christ who died on the cross for you cleanses you from all sin.*)

Thank you Lord, for forgiving me. Show me how to take a stand and to make a permanent decision to live a crucified life in You. Teach me to recognize and identify demons that are at work in my life. Show me their activity and their works in my life and what they force me to do and how they lead me astray. I place my trust in You Lord Jesus. Amen

Now tell every demon that is in the room that you are in, above it, below it, to be bound and powerless, be confused, blinded, and dismayed. Command them not call out to one another, not to render aid to each other or hide behind each other, and to obey your commands in the name of Jesus.

Place your hands over your navel and speak the following:

I break the power of every demon off my life in the name of Jesus Christ and every generational curse that entered me through my stomach when I was attached to my mother through the umbilical cord. Every demon that entered me through my ancestors on my father's side or on my mother's side that came into me through my bloodline, I command you to be bound in the name of Jesus Christ. Every demon all the way back to Adam and Eve on both sides of my family be bound and every curse that followed them be void of your power over my life and my future family generations now in the name of Jesus Christ.

> *"You shall not bow down to them or worship them; for I, the Lord your God, am a jealous God, punishing the children for the sin of the fathers to the third and fourth generation of those who hate Me."* Exodus 20:5 *(See also Exodus 34:7, Numbers 14:18, Deuteronomy 5:9)*

But how can a curse go down more than four generations? Some curses go down to ten generations.

> *One of illegitimate birth shall not enter the assembly of the Lord, even to the tenth generation none of his descendants shall enter the assembly of the Lord.* Deuteronomy 23:2

(NIV Study Bible gives this note: Perhaps forever, since ten is symbolic of completeness or finality) some curses seem to last forever.

Proverbs 17:13 - *"If a man pays back evil for good, evil will never leave his house."*

1 Samuel 2:31- [Word given to Eli] *"The time is coming when I will cut short your strength and the strength of your father's house, so that there will not be an old man in your family line."*

Jeremiah 23:40 - *"I will bring upon you everlasting disgrace – everlasting shame that will not be forgotten."*

2 Samuel 12:10 – [Word given to David] *"Now, therefore, the sword will never depart from your house, because you despised Me and took the wife of Uriah the Hittite to be your own."*

Jesus broke every curse for us

Galatians 3:13 - *Christ has redeemed us from the curse of the law, having become a curse for us (for it is written, "Cursed is everyone who hangs on a tree").*

Jesus broke these curses in His body on the cross – See my book *"Breaking Generational Curses".*

This is why I break generational curses in the name of Jesus that go as far back as Adam and Eve.

As I have explained in a previous chapter, demons come out in the name of Jesus and they come out in a loud voice. There is a lot of breath that is expelled in order to make a loud voice. The Greek word for spirit and breath is the same word *"pneuma"*. When Jesus was casting out spirits a lot of *"pneuma"* was expelled, that is breath/spirit. So in this deliverance, as in the previous chapter, as an act of your will, I will ask you to blow out breath in the name of Jesus to start the process of putting your will behind this deliverance.

Speak the following:

Since the Lord Jesus Christ gave me authority over all the

power of the enemy in Luke 10:19, I now take the authority over every demonic being or structure that has afflicted me. I command every principality, every power, all world forces of darkness, all spiritual forces of wickedness in heavenly places to be powerless in my life and I command your power over my life to be void in my life in Jesus' name, that includes every station, every rank within the demonic kingdom that is responsible for attacks on me and my family, to be void of your power in the name of Jesus Christ.

Every spirit behind disease, calamity, illness, death, temptation, every spirit that attaches to the fleshly desires of the fallen nature and sinfulness, be bound and powerless and void of your powers over me in the name of Jesus Christ. Every spirit that entices me, harasses me, tortures me, torments me, compels me, and enslaves me, addicts me, defiles me, deceives me, and attacks me, be void of your power over me now in the name of Jesus Christ. Now every last one of you and your kindred spirits, leave me now in the name of Jesus.

Now take a deep breath and blow it out, as if it is bad breath.
Go! In the name of Jesus.

Now we are going to cast out evil spirits who have attached themselves to your flesh, emotions, will and intellect.

In the name of Jesus, I command out of me the spirits of:

Abandonment, rejection, feeling forsaken, neglected hurts, cast away, cast aside, widow, orphan, unloved, unwanted.

I command those evil spirits to leave me now in the name of Jesus Christ.

Now take a deep breath and blow out breath. Go! In the

name of Jesus.

In Jesus' name, I command out of me every evil spirit of:

Accidents, calamity, injury, mishap, catastrophe, misfortune, loss. Now take a deep breath and blow out. Go! In the name of Jesus.

In the name of Jesus, I command out of me every spirit of:

Accusation, slander, accuser of the brethren, suspicion, fault finding, jealousy, envy, bitterness, hatred, finger pointing, judging, false accusation.

Now take a deep breath and blow out. Go! In the name of Jesus.

In the name of Jesus, I command out of me every spirit of:

Addiction, compulsion, obsession, alcohol, Bacchus (god of drunkenness) intoxication, drugs, illegal drugs, legal drugs, nicotine, caffeine, sugar, exercise, TV, spendthrift, food cravings, chronic illness, compulsive lying, credit cards, emotional abuse, female dependency, male dependency, fighting, gambling, addicted to love, addicted to money, over-eating, addicted to pain, physical abuse, chasing the opposite or same sex, addicted to sex, sexual abuse, shopping, soap operas, sports, talking, telephone, video games, work, or any other addiction that has me in its grip I command out of me in the name of Jesus Christ.

Now take a deep breath and blow it out. Go! In the name of Jesus Christ.

In the name of Jesus, I command out of me the spirit of:

Anti-Christ; all religious spirits that fight against Jesus

Christ and the truth of the gospel, false teaching, error, blasphemy, arrested development spirits that hinder me from growing into adulthood, by both spiritually and/or are physically blocking my growth, immaturity, hindrance, blockage, obstruction of personality, foolishness, infantile, juvenile, adolescent, bound and blocked personality, anorexia, eating disorders, starvation, death, fear of becoming fat, compulsive dieting, depression, self rejection, low self-esteem, false image.

Now take a deep breath and blow it out. Go! In the name of Jesus.

In the name of Jesus, I command out of me all spirits of:

Attention-getting, attention seeking, playacting, lying, you the one who is over evil spirits, you, the ruling spirit Beelzebub, lord of the flies, spiritual blindness, natural blindness, spiritual dullness, spirit of burdens, heaviness, load, sorrow, false burden, carnality, fleshly, earthly, old man, lewdness, sensuality, worldliness, lust, lasciviousness, immorality, strife, envy, factions, divisions, contemptuous, fighting, discord, pride, corruption, dishonesty, extortion, fraud, depravity, and impurity, perversion, vice, vulgarity, rottenness,

Now take a deep breath and blow it out. Go! In the name of Jesus.

In the name of Jesus, I command out of me all spirits of:

Deception-Lying, false doctrines, false teachings, error, heresy, doctrines of devils, all curses, false religion, false religious movement, falsehood, false love, false personalities, false gifts, false prophecy, false tongues, false revelation, false doctrines, false prophet, false teacher, false church, false anointing, false praise, false worship, false friendship, phony, fake, counterfeit, deception, lying, hypocrisy, Pharisee, dishonesty, flattery, pretense, false religious burdens, false responsibility,

Now take a deep breath and blow out. Go! In the name of Jesus.

In Jesus' name, I command out of me every spirit of:

Depression, failure curses, defeat frustration, discouragement, suicide, depression, sorrow, confusion, rejection, sadness, grief crying, anger, hatred, rage, uncontrollable emotions, hurt.

Now take a deep breath and blow out. Go in the name of Jesus.

In the name of Jesus, I command out of me every spirit of:

Infirmity, Epilepsy, fits, convulsions and seizures every spirit attached to an illness or sickness (name your sickness or your illness), I command that illness out of me now in the name of Jesus Christ. I command it to go and leave me in Jesus name.

Now take a deep breath and blow it out. Go in the name of Jesus Christ.

In the name of Jesus, I command out of me every evil spirit that causes me:

To have no energy, to be tired and to be lazy, forgetful, have memory loss, absent-minded, frigidity, coldness in marriage, spirit that blocks the sex drive, you who punishes my spouse-sex partner, I command the spirit of control by frigidity in the name of Jesus Christ to leave me now. Take a deep breath and blow out! Go in Jesus name.

In the name of Jesus, I command out of me every evil spirit of:

Powerlessness that blocks me, hinders me or obstructs me, the spirit that says to me, no love, no help, no friends, no success, no lodging, no pity, no understanding, no wisdom, no relief, constant torment, no rest, no solution, no power, no ability, no light, always darkness, no healing, no deliverance, no happiness, no joy, no victory, no control, no future, hopelessness, no liberty, no discernment, no prosperity, no breakthrough, no direction, no open doors, no money, no job, no anointing, no blessing, no communication, no growth, no support, no morals, no escape, no commitment, no self-control, no opportunity, no family, no transportation, no mobility, no break, no time, no room, no strength, no home, no vision, and every demon assigned to the curse that says **no** to me.

I command you to go out of my life and away from me in the name of Jesus. Take a deep breath and blow it out. Go in the name of Jesus.

In Jesus' name, I command out of me every demon of:

Stubbornness, headstrong, obstinate, self wilderness, anti-submissive, rebellion, independent, unyielding and every spirit that goes contrary to good/to God, every perverse spirit, idolatry, impulsiveness, rashness, careless, hasty, intellectualism, lack, poverty, insufficiency, lawlessness, criminal minded, disorder, nonconformity, corruption, withdrawal, discontentment, defeatism, hopelessness, death, suicide, insomnia, heaviness, memory flashback, memory recall, bad memories, hurtful memories, painful memories, blocked memories, trauma, denial, Alzheimer's disease, insanity, mental illness, madness, confusion, retardation, mania, senility, schizophrenia, paranoia, and hallucinations go in the name of Jesus. Now take a deep breath and blow it out. Go! In the name of Jesus.

In the name of Jesus, I command out of me every spirit of:

Molestation, abuse, violation, wound, bitterness, anger, guilt, shame, murmuring, whispering, complaining, distress, depression, heavy load, suspicion, mistrust, apprehension, persecution, jealousy, envy, pessimism, cynicism, doubt, disbelief, nightmares, delusions, phantoms spirits, incubus, succubus, irrational fears, fright, panic, dread, fear the future, fear the unknown, fear of losing loved ones, gluttony, pornography, filthy speech, prostitution, rape, rage, rejection, resistant to the truth, resistant to the word, resistant to the Holy Spirit, resistant to salvation, resistance to deliverance, resistance to praise, resistance to worship, resistance to prayers, opposition, stubbornness, hardness of heart, unbelief, rigidness, rudeness, set in your ways, narrow minded, disrespect, arrogance, sharp tongue, harshness, ruthlessness, merciless, sternness, cutthroat, revenge, spirit of vendetta, retaliation, victim spirit, double mindedness, unteachable, playboy, fornication, seducer, Don Juan stud, a Casanova, womanizer, harlot, sleazy, liar, nymphomaniac, immorality, narcissism, self love, self righteous, self exultation, self promotion, self willed, self ruled, self centered, self seeking, egotism, pride, and every like spirit come out of me now in the name of Jesus Christ. Take a deep breath and blow it out. Go in the name of Jesus Christ.

In the name of Jesus Christ I command out of me every spirit of:

Shame, sickness, shyness, strife, contention, arguing, confusion, tale bearing, gossip, laziness, slothfulness, unreality, unworthy, inferiority, worthless, victim, pushover, doormat, sitting duck, pornography, lewdness, lust, perversion, uncleanness, sexual impurity, homosexuality, lesbianism, orgy, lasciviousness, filthiness, prostitution, control, tyrant, dictator, domination slave driver, task master, I command these evil spirits out of me now, in the name of Jesus Christ go! Take a deep breath and blow out. Go!

Here are some final words on this teaching and your deliverance. Many of you who read this and followed along with the deliverance at the end were set free. Let it be known to you that Jesus Christ has set you free and it was the power of His blood that He shed on the cross that won this victory for you. However, it is up to you to keep your healing and deliverance by taking a stand against the enemy who would like to come back and dwell in your fleshly body.

Pray: Lord Jesus, I ask you to come and bring the Holy Spirit and live in these areas that are now vacant and I ask you to take up residence where those demons were. I give those areas to you, Lord Jesus, and now I take a stand against the enemy. When he tries to come back, he will see that I have given You Lordship in those areas. Amen

Chapter 4
Knowing Your Enemy

About one fourth of the ministry of Jesus was casting out demons. In this chapter I will speak about knowing your enemy, and also knowing God. During His brief three and one half year walk on this earth, Jesus did exactly what He declared. We see this statement in the gospel of Luke. Jesus enters the synagogue and began reading aloud from the book of Isaiah.

> *"The Spirit of the LORD is upon Me, Because He has anointed Me To preach the gospel to the poor; He has sent Me to heal the brokenhearted, To proclaim liberty to the captives and recovery of sight to the blind, To set at liberty those who are oppressed;"* Luke 4:18 (NKJV)

Jesus declared his ministry as He quoted from the scroll in Isaiah 61, and then He went around doing exactly what He declared. Family, this ministry was not only for Jesus Christ, but these ministries are for all who are disciples of the Lord Jesus Christ.

Who are disciples of the Lord Jesus Christ? We are! All who have accepted the Lord Jesus Christ as their Savior are His disciples. And His declaration in Luke 4:18 is also for us. Amen!

Before I explain to you about knowing your enemy I would like to share with you the many ways to be delivered.

1. The Word of God is a healing and delivering word.

> *Psalm 107:20: He sent His word and healed them, and delivered them from their destructions.*

By reading the Bible you can be healed and delivered and set free. One scripture that shows how you can be delivered is found in; James 4:7-8, *Therefore* **submit** *therefore to God,* **resist** *the devil and he will flee from you.* ***Draw near*** *to God and He will draw near to you.*

There are three steps in this deliverance passage. The first is **submission to God**. Many times there is no deliverance because people do not want to submit their lives to God. The second step in this passage is to **resist the devil**. A lot of people can't receive their deliverance, because they won't say NO to the devil. Just say NO to him. The third step in this scripture is **draw near to God**. Many who are locked into a sinful life are so filled with condemnation that they can not see the love of a forgiving Father, so they run from God instead of drawing near to Him.

We should take the example of King David who was a sinner just like us. Even though he did terrible sins, he drew close to God for forgiveness and freedom from condemnation. No matter what the bondage, Family, draw near to God. Don't run and hide in shame.

2. Calling upon the name of the Lord

Romans 10:13 tells us that *"whoever will **call upon the Name of the Lord** shall be saved."* The word **saved,** found in Vines Complete Expository Dictionary, comes from the Greek word "sozo" It is an all inclusive word meaning, salvation, healing, and deliverance from bondage. In other words, you are going to be made whole when you **call upon the name of the Lord Jesus Christ** – completely whole. But you must have faith in Him when calling upon His name for healing, salvation and deliverance.

> *But without faith it is impossible to please him: for he that **cometh** to God must believe that he is, and that he is a **rewarder** of them that diligently seek him.* Hebrews 11:6 (KJV)

3. Casting out demons:

> *And these signs will follow those who believe: In My name they will cast out demons; they will speak with*

new tongues; they will take up serpents; and if they drink anything deadly, it will by no means hurt them; they will lay hands on the sick, and they will recover." Mark 16:17-18 (NKJV)

This is a declaration and a command from Jesus Christ to all believers. Notice that the first sign is the casting out of demons. If you are a believer you should cast out demons starting with yourself first. Get yourself free first before you try to free up others.

4. Die to the old self-centered life

Gal.2:20 I have been crucified with Christ; it is no longer I who live, but Christ lives in me; and the life which I now live in the flesh I live by faith in the Son of God, who loved me and gave Himself for me.

Die to the old carnal appetites. About 90% of our problems are caused by demons pushing us to live a carnal life. People want to live in carnality and the demons want us to live in it also so we will be constantly in sin.

Deliverance from demons is possible through Jesus Christ, but deliverance from the flesh is impossible. The flesh, our carnal self- driven desires, must be crucified. It is an act of will.

5. Praise and worship

Let the saints exult in glory: Let them sing for joy upon their beds. Let the high praises of God be in their mouth, And a two- edged sword in their hand; To execute vengeance upon the nations, And punishments upon the peoples; To bind their kings with chains, And their nobles with fetters of iron; To execute upon them the judgment written: This honor have all his saints. Praise ye Jehovah. Psalm 149:5-9 (NASV)

When we praise the Lord, we are binding principalities and powers executing judgment on them. Notice that all His saints (we) have that honor.

6. Hands trained for war

Blessed be the Lord my rock who trains my hands for war, and my fingers for battle. Psalm. 144:1 (NKJV)

In **Mark 16:17**, Jesus told us: ***they will lay hands on the sick, and they will recover."*** Our hands are for spiritual war and for healing according to the word. (For more information, please get my CD on the laying on of hands)

7. Prayer Cloths

Now God worked unusual miracles by the hand of Paul, 12 so that even handkerchiefs or aprons were brought from his body to the sick and the diseases left them and the evil spirits went out of them. Acts 19:11-12 (NKJV)

I have heard testimonies of people being healed by receiving a prayer cloth and demons fled just like the scripture said they would. A prayer cloth is any piece of cloth that is sent to the sick or the demonized with the intent of activating the above scripture. It is intended for healing and deliverance only and not for any other purpose. Any other purpose would make it a good luck charm or an amulet. Make sure this is made crystal clear when sending it to the sick and the demonized.

In deliverance there are three things we seek to accomplish:

1. Cast Out Demons

First of all we are to recognize and expel demon spirits from the bodies of men, women, children, even animals and houses. There are many ways to set the captives free.

My wife and I were called to a house to pray over it because strange things were happening in the home and the owners felt the presence of darkness. We prayed until I came to a picture on the wall, that their daughter had painted, and the Holy spirit prompted me to tell them to take it down and when they opened the back of it, it revealed a hidden picture of a poster of a rock band called "KISS" (Knights in Satan's Service"). Then we commanded the evil spirits out of the house.

2. Learn how to stay free

Following deliverance we offer instructions to those who were set free on how to stay free. It is very easy to deliver people from demons in the name of Jesus, by the power of the Holy Spirit. But to maintain a deliverance is something that the delivered has to do. I can not do that for you. I can command demons to go, but it is up to you to hold onto it.

The devil will always come and try to rob you of the deliverance that you have received, or of the healing that you have received. Some people have been prayed for healing and received it and a few hours later, the symptoms are back again. Why? You are being robbed of your healing. That is the time to go into spiritual warfare.

When that happens, don't be passive. YOU tell them to get out of your life. Say this to the devil, "You, the one who is robbing me of my healing, get out of me in the name of Jesus. Start waging warfare on those demons who are attempting to lay those symptoms back on you.

After you have been delivered, you are in a new position. You have to come to the part in the Bible (Eph 6:13) where it says

...and having done all, to stand. Vs. 14. **Stand therefore.** *Stand therefore (hold your ground), having tightened the belt of truth around your loins and having put on the breastplate of integrity and of moral rectitude and right standing with God,* (AMP)

A great illustration is asking someone to hand you something, and taking it in your hand, asking them to hand it to you again. I am sure that the person who handed it to you would say something like, "I already handed it to you.

Don't let the enemy steal it away from you."

This is the way we are to look at deliverance. We have received deliverance from demons in Jesus' name. When delivered, we don't need to get delivered again, but believe we **were** delivered and stand in that deliverance. Having done all, to stand. Stand therefore.

In the back of my father's book "Eight Keys to Spiritual and Physical Health," there is a chapter devoted on how to keep your healing and deliverance, 15 ways. I suggest you get the book and read it.

3. Point the Person to Jesus

The third thing we are seeking to do is to give support to those who are in this spiritual warfare. After deliverance there are times when the person who had deliverance needs additional prayers and that I do gladly, always pointing that person to Jesus the deliverer. Problems arise when people rely on the minister to deliver them instead of trusting the Lord Jesus to deliver them. When this happens, it is important to help the person refocus his position of faith in Jesus for receiving his full deliverance so that he will not rely on a minister. Train them to place their faith in a Jesus position instead of a man position. For some this will be easy; for others it is harder. Faith has to be built in Jesus not man.

> *Wherefore, my beloved, as ye have always obeyed, not as in my presence only, but now much more in my absence,* ***work out*** *your own* ***salvation*** *with fear and trembling.* Philippians 2:12(NKJV)

I often used this passage for telling people that they needed to work to keep their salvation; that is their eternal life, but I always felt conviction when I said that. It was a contradiction to what the Word said in Ephesians 2:8-9:

"For by grace are ye saved through faith; and that not

of yourselves: it is the gift of God: Not of works, lest any man shall boast."

So then what does it mean here in Philippians 2:12 when it says, *"work out your own salvation with fear and trembling?"* I looked up the word salvation used in this passage in Strong's Concordance #4991 the Greek word for salvation in this passage is sōtēria (sō-tā-rē'-ä) It literally means deliverance, preservation, safety, salvation; deliverance from the molestation of enemies.

Scripture describes a fourfold salvation: saved from the penalty, power, presence and the pleasure of sin. (cf. Arthur W. Pink, *A Fourfold Salvation*)

In this case, the word salvation (sōtēria) means deliverance from the power of the enemy. So in this passage it means and should read "work" out your **deliverance** with fear and trembling.

So, going back over what I said earlier, in giving support to those who are in the battle of deliverance, first I pray for them and then I direct them to Jesus for their deliverance and if they need more after that, I redirect them in their faith towards Jesus, and let them know that they are at the place in the Bible, Ephesians 6:13 where it says ..."*and having done all, to stand.* V. 14. **Stand therefore.**"

Supporting those in deliverance means teaching those who were delivered how to work out their deliverance by standing in their faith, in their deliverance. That is, teaching them to trust the deliverance that Jesus gave them instead of deliverance of what man gave them.

Know the one who gives you victory. It is Jesus Christ.

And Jesus came and spoke to them, saying, "All authority has been given to Me in heaven and on earth". Matthew 28:18 (NKJV)

An interesting note is that Jesus hands us believers

authority over **all** the power of the enemy. He said: *"Behold, I give you the authority to trample on serpents and scorpions, and over all the power of the enemy, and nothing shall by any means hurt you".* Luke 10:19 (NKJV)

We have been given power over ALL - ALL - ALL the power of the enemy!

This is vital! You are operating under the authority of Jesus when casting demons out in His name, and nothing will harm you. You have to understand this in order to be delivered and to deliver others. Learn to use your authority.

Most of us do not fully understand our authority because we do not understand who is in us. The Bible says in 1 John 4:4 *Ye are of God, little children, and have overcome them: because **greater is He that is in you, than he that is in the world.*** **(KJV)**

Proclaim this aloud. Say, *"Greater is He that is in me than he that is in the world".* Who is in the world? The devil. Who is in you? The Holy Spirit. The same Spirit that raised Christ from the dead dwells in you (Rom. 8:11). We have overcome the world, because the Holy Spirit is in us. Therefore, as it says in Romans 8:37-40:

Yet in all these things we are more than conquerors through Him who loved us. 38 For I am persuaded that neither death nor life, nor angels nor principalities nor powers, nor things present nor things to come, 39 nor height nor depth, nor any other created thing, shall be able to separate us from the love of God which is in Christ Jesus our Lord. (NKJV)

Now one of the important issues in deliverance and the receiving of deliverance is that we do not compromise. Remember what Jesus said in Matt. 12:30, *you are either for me or against me.* There is no middle ground. Some Christians want to see how much they can get away with before it becomes sin; how far can they go. Family, there is no compromising with the Lord Jesus Christ.

> *When the Lord your God brings you into the land which you go to possess, and has cast out many nations before you, the Hittites and the Girgashites and the Amorites and the Canaanites and the Perizzites and the Hivites and the Jebusites, seven nations greater and mightier than you, and when the Lord your God delivers them over to you, you shall conquer them and utterly destroy them. You shall make no covenant with them nor show mercy to them.* Deuteronomy 7:1-2 (NKJV)

We need to be aware how demons operate, how the mind is attacked, and what demons are working in that person; and we must not compromise with demons.

Many times in deliverance, I seek to find out if the person is presently engaging in some form of sin, such as an unmarried couple living together, adultery, occultism, stealing, etc. For an effective deliverance, all sins must be renounced and turned away from or else those sins, become a bridge to all those cast out demons to cross back over into their lives. Compromising and keeping sin in our lives is much like posting a road sign up for the demons, saying, "This way back in."

> *When an unclean spirit goes out of a man, he goes through dry places, seeking rest, and finds none. Then he says, 'I will return to my house from which I came.' And when he comes, he finds it empty, swept, and put in order. Then he goes and takes with him seven other spirits more wicked than himself, and they enter and dwell there; and the last state of that man is worse than the first.* Matthew 12:43-45 (NKJV)

For a detailed explanation, please get my CD on "When A Spirit Goes Out Of A Man." Family, it is extremely important to destroy all doorways or bridges of sin so the enemy will not have a way back into your lives. Demons know what you think because they operate in your mind. They are the ones who plant the thoughts and plans of sin for you to run with.

An uncompromised life sounds like this, "Lord, I want You and only You. Show me if there is any evil way in me, any sin in my life, so I may cast it out." That is the attitude of an uncompromised life in Christ. If you drink to get drunk, stop it!

If you smoke, stop it. If you curse, stop it. If you cheat, stop it. If you lie, stop it, If you steal, stop it. If you sin sexually, stop it. If you continually sin in any way, stop it. Stop making bridges for the devil to re-enter your life. Stop not just sinful actions but also sinful attitudes.

Paul warned the Corinthians about unforgiveness in 2 Cor. 2:11

*lest Satan should take advantage of us; for we are not ignorant of his **devices.***

I did a word search from the Interlinear Bible that translates each word from Greek to give the English meaning. The Greek word for **device** is " noema" pronounced "No-a-ma" it also gave the Strong's concordance reference for the purpose of that word used in this passage Strong's #3540 it means: 1.) a mental perception, thought; 2.) an evil purpose; 3.) that which thinks, the mind, thoughts or purposes.

So, this scripture is saying to us something like this, "We should not let Satan take advantage of us; for we are not ignorant of his mental perception, his thoughts, his evil purpose.

You see family, Satan will try to plant a mental perception and thoughts of evil in our minds and we should not be ignorant of this. You have to recognize that those are his evil plans for your life. Satan's thoughts are sometimes disguised to seem like your own thoughts. If you agree with them and receive them as your own thoughts, you will fall prey to Satan's schemes. Pray for God's wisdom and discernment and how to use your spiritual weapons.

> *For though we walk in the flesh, we do not war according to the flesh. For the weapons of our warfare are not carnal but mighty in God for **pulling down strongholds,** casting down arguments and every high thing that exalts itself against the knowledge of God, bringing every thought into captivity to the obedience of Christ,* 2 Corinthians 10:3-5 (NKJV)

In the Literal Greek/English (Interlinear) Vs.5 reads demolish strongholds, imaginations demolishing, every high thing lifted up against the knowledge of God. There are **three things** we need to look at in this passage.

1. The words casting down or pulling down literally means to **demolish.** Think of what that word means. It means to smash, tear down, to destroy.

We are to smash, tear down, and destroy **strongholds** which are enemy forts in our minds. These are thought patterns called paradigms, circumstances of our lives, that is how we view life through our wounds, and misfortunes. The enemy can set up a twisted view of ourselves and life in our minds.

2. The **imaginations** are those thoughts that build these forts of the wounded and twisted mind. Those imaginations need to be smashed, torn down, demolished. They need to be replaced with new thinking, a new mind. For instance……..Start thinking about the pleasant things and good time that happened with people or things around the time of those instances. Try in every way to get past the wounds.

I remember when I was a young lad and I was riding my bike down the road in front of my house. They had dug up the street and there was coral rock everywhere. I was going very fast when my bike broke apart at the front fork and I went flying. I suffered a severe cut on one of my toes. South Florida boys all went barefoot back then. Some of the coral rock went deep into the wound and my toe took years to heal properly.

To this day, my toe and toenail are a little scarred. I see my toe every morning when I put my socks on. For a long time I was mad at that bike for breaking apart. I could still be mad at that bike for breaking apart if I hadn't changed my thinking. After all, I see that wound every day. If I had worn shoes, it wouldn't have happened. Since I couldn't go back and change that, I changed, demolished, and smashed the thought of that wound by remembering what a great bike that was. It was the best riding bike I ever owned. It had the greatest balance. You see, Family, I changed a paradigm, a thought pattern by replacing it with new thoughts of truth.

*For the **mind** set on the flesh is death, but the **mind** set on the*
***Spirit** is life and peace,* Romans 8:6 (NASB)

*...that, in reference to your former manner of life, you lay aside the old self, which is being corrupted in accordance with the lusts of deceit, and that you be renewed in **the spirit of your mind**, and put on the new self, which in the likeness of God has been created in righteousness and holiness of the **truth**.* Ephesians 4:22-24 (NASB)

A fleshly mind is a mind that is in a **twisted or wounded imagination**. It is death. A **new mind**, "renewed in the spirit of the mind" is something that is created by you, in righteousness and the holiness of **the truth. Say that aloud – "the truth."**

You see, Family, when you tear down those paradigms of strongholds, and the imaginations that built them, they must be replaced by a mind renewed in **truth.** The thought patterns of lies from the enemy need to be changed from lies, to truth.

You have to know that you have the weapons of warfare and you have to know where the warfare is located. It is located in your mind. The battle is in your mind. This is where the enemy has his strongholds. There is constant warfare going on right there in your mind. I think I'm going to do it. – No, I think I won't. – I think I can get away with it. – I don't think anyone will see me. – I'll try it, they won't know.

We all try to justify sin and we know it is wrong. There is constant temptation and warfare going on in our minds, sometimes even when we are praying or singing to the Lord, the most ungodly thoughts enter our minds. We can see from the very beginning by what God told Cain that sin is always there, and it must be conquered.

> *"If you do well, will not your countenance be lifted up? And if you do not do well, sin is **crouching** at the door; and its desire is for you, but you must master it."* Genesis 4:7 (NASB)

> *...Then when lust has conceived, it gives birth to **sin**; and when*
> ***sin** is accomplished, it brings forth **death**.* James 1:15 (NASB)

We have to pull down those ungodly thoughts. Let me teach you what I do when this happens to me, I say something like this:

> I command my mind to come into obedience in the name of Jesus Christ and bring every thought captive to the obedience of Jesus Christ. I pull down every stronghold of the enemy in Jesus' name. I command the spirits of those ungodly thoughts to be bound and powerless in Jesus' name. I command you to leave my mind, you, the one that makes me think of......name what it is doing in my mind, and repeat, "You go! Leave my mind now in Jesus' name.

Then after you have done that, you must purposely change

your thought pattern. Start worshiping the Lord. Think of something good about the Lord.

How can we build Godly strongholds and replace the ungodly strongholds?

1. Read the Bible

2. Listen to Godly music

3. Watch Godly TV and movies

Finally, my brothers, whatever things are true, whatever things are honest, whatever things are right, whatever things are pure, whatever things are lovely, whatever things are of good report; if there is any virtue and if there is any praise, **think on these things***.* Philippians 4:8 (MKJV)

Know your weapons of warfare:

1. The name of Jesus In the name of Jesus we can ask the Father for our needs. In the name of Jesus, we can bind the power of darkness. In the name of Jesus we can cast out demons. In the name of Jesus we can heal the sick and raise the dead. The name of Jesus is the most powerful name ever. There is no other name given by which men must be saved. It is in Jesus' name.

2. The blood of the Lamb and the word of our testimony, **Rev. 12:11.** I have learned over time that it is important to apply the blood of Jesus to my prayers more and more. I cover myself and my family and possessions with the precious blood of Jesus before and after battle. Even while praying for others, I claim the blood of Jesus over them and their families, possessions, and employment.

3. **The word of our testimony.** It is important to share your testimony before men. That is one way to become and to remain healed and delivered. Tell people how the Lord has set you free. Let them know the bondage Satan had you in and let them know how Jesus set you free. It's your

testimony.

I had a hard time explaining my personal testimony for a couple of years. I didn't know how to format it into a victory report. I just knew I was free of certain bondages and I couldn't articulate it to others clearly. I prayed and asked the Lord to show me how to tell others of my testimony without sounding like a fool; and He did. I heard someone give an "elevator testimony." That is to say, they gave their testimony in the time it takes to get from the first floor to the sixth floor (about 30 seconds). In that time they gave the front, middle and ending of their testimony. That was my model to use from then on. I cut out all the things that would raise eyebrows and make me look like a nut and just put the facts down in my testimony. Here is my elevator testimony in about 30 seconds.

> God sent Jesus Christ, His only begotten son, to die on the cross for my sins, but I rejected Him up until I was 27 yrs. old. Then one day, conviction of my sins became evident to me. For the first time in my life, I was afraid of dying and being judged for my sins. I surrendered myself and all my ways to Jesus Christ and **I accepted the payment He made for me on the cross with His life. He paid for my sins, and I am forgiven. Now I am restored back into a personal relationship with our heavenly Father.** *(What Jesus has purchased for me is the **essence** of my testimony)*

Now, it was much more involved than that. I could write you 10 pages of details, and coincidences that are intimate and personal to me. These are things that happened between me and the Lord that brought me to salvation. All of those things are also part of my testimony, but if I included them, it would take you off track of the main testimony.

4. The Word of God. Use the Word of God against the enemy as Jesus did. *Matthew 4:1-11* (NASB)

Then Jesus was led up by the Spirit into the wilderness

to be tempted by the devil. And after He had fasted forty days and forty nights, He then became hungry. And the tempter came and said to Him, "If You are the Son of God, command that these stones become bread."

But He answered and said, **"It is written,** *'*MAN SHALL NOT LIVE ON BREAD ALONE, BUT ON EVERY WORD THAT PROCEEDS OUT OF THE MOUTH OF GOD.'"

Then the devil took Him into the holy city and had Him stand on the pinnacle of the temple, and said to Him, "If You are the Son of God, throw Yourself down; for it is written, He will command His angels concerning You and on their hands they will bear You up, so that You will not strike Your foot against a stone.'"

*Je*sus said to him, "On the other hand, **it is written,** 'YOU SHALL NOT PUT THE LORD YOUR GOD TO THE TEST.'"

Again, the devil took Him to a very high mountain and showed Him all the kingdoms of the world and their glory; and he said to Him, "All these things I will give You, if You fall down and worship me."

Then Jesus said to him, "Go, Satan! For it **is written,** 'YOU SHALL WORSHIP THE LORD YOUR GOD, AND SERVE HIM ONLY.'"

Then the <u>devil left Him;</u> and behold, angels came and began to minister to Him.

    We are to do what Jesus did when the devil came at him. He quoted scripture at him and the enemy left Him. When you feel unsaved and when the enemy makes you feel unworthily, quote scriptures at him

I am saved by grace through faith. (Eph. 2:8) I am forgiven (Col. 1:13 14),

I am redeemed from the hand of the enemy (Ps.107:2); I am justified (Rom. 5:1);

I am redeemed from the curse of the law (Gal. 3:13);

I am a child of God (Rom. 8:16); I am a son of God (Rom. 8:14);

I am an heir of God and joint heir with Jesus (Rom. 8:17).

Declare what scripture says about who you are and what you can do. Quote those verses and the enemy will leave you also.

Get the Word of God in you. You have to know the Word of God and quote it. Everyone has their favorite quotations. I am challenging you to add more quotation to your bible knowledge every day. Get strong in His Word.

Sometimes people ask me "What are demons?" "Where do they come from?" Demons are evil spirits without bodies who seek bodies to operate in and through to express themselves, in their desire to fight against God and against those whom God loves. The Bible tells us that evil angels (demons) fell with Satan.

And war broke out in heaven: Michael and his angels fought with the dragon; and the dragon and his angels fought. but they did not prevail, nor was a place found for them in heaven any longer. So the great dragon was cast out, that serpent of old, called the Devil and Satan, who deceives the whole world; he was cast to the earth, and his angels were cast out with him. Then I heard a loud voice saying in heaven, "Now salvation, and strength, and the kingdom of our God, and the power of His Christ have come, for the accuser of our brethren, who accused them before our God day and night, has been cast down. And they (the brethren) overcame him (Satan) by the blood of the Lamb and by the word of their testimony, and they did not love their lives to the death. Revelation 12:7-11 (NKJV)

Family, Satan is not confined in hell. He has not been put there as of yet. He roams the earth seeking whom he may devour (1 Peter 5:8) and he also accuses the saints day and night Rev. 12:10). Even though he was kicked out of heaven, he accuses us before God in the spiritual realm. Satan's angels are demons and they are his evil agents.

Demons have all the attributes of a human soul.

In Matthew 12:43 we read that the spirit that was cast out says I will return to my house. And in the case of the demons who were cast into the swine (Matt 8:31), they chose where to go. Demons have a will; an intellect to choose. Demons fear and tremble. They have emotions, as we read in James 2:19 (NKJV): *You believe that there is one God. You do well. Even the demons believe—and tremble!*

They have knowledge

Now there was a man in their synagogue with an unclean spirit. And he cried out, 24 saying, "Let us alone! What have we to do with You, Jesus of Nazareth? Did You come to destroy us? I know who You are—the Holy One of God!" Mark 1:23-24 (NKJV)

They have self awareness

"My name is Legion." Mark 5:9. They knew who they were and how many were present. *"Let us alone! What have we to do with You, Jesus of Nazareth."* Mark 1:24 -They have ability to speak

"These men are the servants of the Most High God, who proclaim to us the way of salvation." Acts 16:17 They can prognosticate or foretell the future which is the counterfeit

of the Holy Spirit's gift of prophecy. So they have wills, intellect, knowledge, emotions, self awareness and the ability to speak. Everything a human soul has.

There are different kinds of demons.

Some demons cause more wickedness than others. Matt. 12:45, *"Then he (the evil spirit) goes and takes with him seven other spirits more wicked than himself."* Some demons need to be cast out after prayer and fasting. Jesus said in Mark 9:29, *"This kind can come out by nothing but prayer and fasting."*(NKJV). Some demons seem to be harder to get cast out than others. You need to pray for insight from God and ask Him for His strategy for them to go. You also might need to have one or two others to stand with you.

Next, we are going to cast out all unclean, evil, demonic spirits that have afflicted you, harassed you, and influenced you. They come out in the name of Jesus and they come out in the breath. When Jesus cast them out, they came out in a loud voice. There is a lot of breath that is expelled in order to make a loud voice. An interesting thing is that in the "Vines Complete Expository Dictionary" the Greek word for spirit and breath is the same word, *"pneuma"*. When Jesus was casting out spirits a lot of *"pneuma"* was expelled, that is breath/spirit. As I have asked you to do in previous chapters, as an act of your will, I will ask you to blow out breath in the name of Jesus to start the process of (evil) "spirits" leaving.

But first, God may be tugging on your heart and you want to have a closer relationship with Him. He is calling you and you feel Him calling you.

Pray aloud the following:
Thank you Heavenly Father for sending Jesus. I want a closer walk with you. Lord, Jesus, I accept you as my Savior, my God, and my King. You died on the cross and were resurrected from the dead. You saved me and

redeemed me with your precious blood. I belong to you, and surrender my whole life to you from this day forward. Please forgive me of all my sins especially any that involved familiar spirits. I renounce and separate myself from all my sinful ways. I call upon you, Lord, to deliver me from the lies and deception of the enemy. And now I take the authority that was given to me by Jesus Christ when he said in Luke 10:19 *"Behold, I have given you authority to tread on serpents and scorpions, and over all the power of the enemy, and nothing will injure you."*

And now according to Matt. 18:18, I command all evil spirits to be bound and powerless in my life, and to loose themselves from me in Jesus' name. I command them not to call out to each other, not to render aid to each other, to unlink themselves from one another and to come out of me now in Jesus' name.

I cover myself from head to toe with the precious blood of Jesus Christ and put on the armor of God.

> *Finally, my brethren, be strong in the Lord and in the power of His might. Put on the whole armor of God, that you may be able to stand against the wiles of the devil. For we do not wrestle against flesh and blood, but against principalities, against powers, against the rulers of the darkness of this age, against spiritual hosts of wickedness in the heavenly places.*
>
> *Therefore take up the whole armor of God, that you may be able to withstand in the evil day, and having done all, to stand. **Stand therefore**, having girded your <u>waist with truth</u>, having put on the <u>breastplate of righteousness,</u> and having shod your <u>feet with the preparation of the gospel of peace</u>; above all, taking the <u>shield of faith</u> with which you will be able to quench all the fiery darts of the wicked one.*
>
> *And take the <u>helmet of salvation</u>, and the <u>sword of the Spirit,</u> <u>which is the word of God</u>; praying always with*

all prayer and supplication in the Spirit, being watchful to this end with all perseverance and supplication for all the saints. Ephesians 6:10-18 (NKJV)

I may repeat the names and activities of some demons because they fall and work in different family groupings. Sometimes this is necessary in order to dislodge them.

Speak aloud the following:

Every spirit that causes me...

Covetousness, self love, love for money, love for power, lust of the world, looking for respectability, self importance, Kleptomania, greed, material lust, idolatry, deception, error, spirits that lie to me and cause me to lie, spirits that sit on my ears telling me lies, spirits of confusion, self deception, perverse spirit, failure, poverty, cheating, conspiracy, I command them out of me now in Jesus' name. Take a deep breath and blow it out. Go in Jesus' name.

In the name of Jesus, I command out of me every spirit of:

Bondage that keeps me tied down to Satan's desires. I renounce these spirits and I command out of me all spirits of **addiction**, addiction to drugs, tobacco, alcohol, food, gluttony, obesity, compulsion, nervous habits, spirits that make me bite my nails, nervousness, insecurity, inferiority, Leave me in the name of Jesus. Take a deep breath and blow it out. Go in Jesus' name

.

In the name of Jesus Christ, I command out of me, every spirit that make me feel:

Unloved, unwanted, insecure, spirits that make me feel unworthy, unaccepted, overly responsible, attention seeking, promiscuity, rape, incest, adultery, sexual deviation, sexual perversion, feeling controlled, repression from abusive authority, addiction to drugs, alcohol, tobacco, sorcery, loneliness, double mindedness, stubbornness, perverse spirit. Take a deep breath and blow it out. Go in Jesus' name.

In the name of Jesus Christ, I command out of me every spirit of:

Deception, drawing the wrong conclusions in error from teachings, from movies, from the internet, from demons, error that comes in from any which way, stubbornness, headstrong, obstinate, strong willed, arrogant, self-willed, self centered, anti-submissive, rebellion, independent, unyielding, contrary, opposite, control, lawless, carnal minded, nonconformity, criminal-minded, hardness of heart. Take a deep breath and blow it out. Go in Jesus' name.

In the name of Jesus Christ, I command out of me every spirit of:

Incubus and Succubus, spirits that have sex with me in my dreams or when I am awake, all evil spirits that have attached to me from an ungodly soul ties. I break the hold of ungodly soul ties with ex-sex partners, especially the soul tie I had with (name the person or persons). I break the hold of their spirit over me now in Jesus' name and command the spirit of that soul tie to leave me now in Jesus' name. Take a deep breath and blow it out. Go, in Jesus' name.

In the name of Jesus, I also break the soul ties with:

Ungodly people: with ungodly leaders, with ungodly friends, people who led me into drugs, or occultism, blood brothers, or sisters, hypnotist, or occult practitioner, ungodly soul ties with people that we love and admire who bring an ungodly controlling spirit. Take a deep breath and blow it out. Go, in Jesus' name.

Let me explain how a person can have an ungodly relationship with a godly person. A person may have an ungodly soul tie with a godly person such as a minister or father who loves them but at the same time controls them. Or a person may worship them and make them an idol. That would represent an ungodly soul tie with a godly person.

In the name of Jesus Christ, I command out of me:

All spirits of idolatry when I bowed my knee to the worshiping of false gods, idol worship, occultism, saint worship, Mary worship, other gods, false doctrines, false religions, devil worship, demon worship, the worship of power, man pleasing spirit, false theologies, false gospels, another gospel, another Jesus, Free Masonry, Eastern Star, witchcraft, bondage, control, Antichrist, spirits that come from all the practices of the East, martial arts, (name the one you were involved in). Take a deep breath and blow it out. Go in Jesus' name.

In the name of Jesus Christ, I command out of me all spirits of:

False religions and all spirits of false practices, all spirits of Voodoo, Buddhism, Santeria, Palo Mayombe, Palero Macumba, Rastafarian, Jehovah Witnesses, Unitarianism, Reiki, Shamanism, Hinduism, Islam, I Ching, or any other religion that does not accept the blood of Jesus Christ as the only atonement for our sins, and the only way to the Heavenly Father, come out of me now in Jesus' name. Take a deep breath and blow it out now. Go in Jesus' name.

In the name of Jesus Christ, I command out of me every spirit of: **Divination,** fortune telling, python, serpent spirits, familiar spirits, spirit guides, Transcendental Meditation, yoga, and the gods of yoga, (Brahma, Vishnu, and Shiva), take with you the serpent spirit that coils at the base of the spine, the spirits of the charkas, and the spirit of the third eye, go! I command you to leave me now in Jesus' name. Take a deep breath and blow it out now in Jesus' name. Go in Jesus' name.

In the name of Jesus Christ, I command out of me all occult spirits:

Divination from spiritists, mediums, palm readers, readers of the future using: cards, crystals, crystal balls, mirrors, twigs, branches, water witching, tea leaves, oil and water, wizards, witchcraft, that operates outside the church, charismatic witchcraft that operates inside the church (not to be confused with true charismatic gifting from God), Voodoo, Shamans who call spirits into themselves, parlor games such as Ouija Board, or occult role playing games such as Dungeons and Dragons, occult movies, occult cartoons. I command you to leave me now in Jesus' name. Go! In Jesus' name. Take a deep breath and blow it out now in Jesus' name. Go in Jesus' name.

In the name of Jesus Christ, I command out of me all occult spirits of:

Acupuncture, Ahab, astral projection, astrology, auras, automatic handwriting, birth signs, black magic, white magic, charms, clairvoyance, colorology, conjuring, crystal balls, curses, enchantment, wizard, warlock, covens, druids, murder, 666, Antichrist, abortion, baby sacrifice, fetishes, lucky charms, fire gazing. Take a deep breath and blow it out now in Jesus' name. Go in Jesus' name.

In the name of Jesus Christ, I command out of me every spirit of:

E.S.P., mental telepathy, soul power, future telling from the devil, warlock, sorcerer, wizard, conjurer, magician, medicine man, soothsayer, necromancy, diviner, spiritual whoredom, spirit of the world, all spirits that came into me through drugs, the lyrics of (demonic or otherwise) music, games, toys, cartoons.

Take a deep breath and blow it out. Go in Jesus' name.

In the name of Jesus Christ, I command out of me every spirit of:

Fortunetelling, I command out of me every spirit that came in through readings of tarot cards, of reading of the rhythm of your body, of oils and waters, of feathers, of twigs, of crystals, of bones, of fortune cookies, horoscopes, birth signs, birth stones, or any new age practice of reading your future or reading your health. Take a deep breath and blow it out now in Jesus' name. Go in Jesus' name.

In the name of Jesus Christ, I command out of me every spirit that came in through:

Handwriting analysis, hexing, horoscopes, hypnosis, idolatry, incantations, levitation, consulting a medium, mental telepathy, E.S.P., mind reading, mind control, soul power, Necromancy, pendulum, pentagram, poltergeist, psychic powers, psychic healers, Reiki, the name of the dead saint you were named after, the name of the dead person you were named after,

Take a deep breath and blow it out now in Jesus' name. Go in Jesus' name.

In the name of Jesus Christ, I command out of me every spirit that came from:

Satan worship, séances, sorcery, (drug use, name the drugs you used), soul travel spells, spirit guides, superstition, table tipping. Take a deep breath and blow it out now in Jesus' name. Go in Jesus' name.

NOTE: I am repeating some demons because they are in more than one category.

In the name of Jesus Christ, I command out of me every spirit that came in through:

Witchcraft, trances, third eye, vexes, voodoo, white magic, black magic, conjuring spirits, premonitions, prognostication, predictions, (making it come to pass by the word you received from the enemy and announcing it as if coming from the Lord) mirror witching or reading, cabala, Wicca, satanism, spirit healers, spiritists, multiple personalities, Disassociative Identity Disorder, ritual abuse, spirits that came in through traumas that cause switching to another you. Multiple Personality Disorder, Disassociation Disorder

Take a deep breath and blow it out now in Jesus' name. Go in Jesus' name.

In the name of Jesus Christ, I command out of me every spirit that came in through:

Fairy tales, reincarnation, karma, yin–yang, spirits of the eastern religions or practices, trances, jinx, spirit of Lucifer, elemental spirits, mystic eye, numerology, pentagram, control, spirit of good luck, bad luck, water witching, omens, secretive, hidden, mysterious secret societies chants, potions, black mass, religious spirits, legalism, charms, good luck charms, ankhs, crooked horns, four leaf clover, or anything you hold for good luck. Take a deep breath and blow it out now in Jesus' name. Go in Jesus' name.

I command the spirit that sits at the gate of my brain. The one that controls the spirit of the mind – You, the one that sits at the seat of my emotion, will, and intellect; You, the one that controls those areas and give me the wrong signals, leave me now. Go in Jesus' name. Take a deep breath and blow it out now in Jesus' name. Go in Jesus' name.

In the name of Jesus Christ, I command out of me all spirits of:

Torment, physical, emotional, mental torment, all spirits of fear. Especially the spirits of fear of: (name your own fears), depression, self pity, despair, loneliness, escapism, hopelessness, discouragement, suicide, spirit of death, pretension, unreality, fantasizing, day dreaming. I command those demons to leave me now. Take a deep breath and blow it out. Go in the name of Jesus.

In the name of Jesus, I command out of me all spirits of:

Compulsion, all spirits that drive me, spirits that cause me to do things I don't want to do, and I command out of me all spirits of perfection, intolerance, pressure, tension, hyperactivity, workaholic, impatience, and all like spirits. I command those demons to leave me now. Take a deep breath and blow it out. Go in Jesus' name.

In the name of Jesus, I command out of me all spirits

That defile me; spirits of lust, fantasy lust, adultery, fornication, sex with spirits, sex with animals, perversion, whoredom, prostitution, incest, abortion, and all defiling spirits. Go in Jesus' name. Take a deep breath and let it out. I command those demons to leave me now and not to enter me any more in Jesus' name.

Now let's invite Jesus and the Holy Spirit into those areas. Say aloud:

> **Dear Lord Jesus, I ask you to come and bring the Holy Spirit and live in these areas that are now vacant and take the place of all these demons that we have commanded out. I give those areas to You, Lord Jesus. Amen**

Chapter 5
Pulling Down Strongholds

In this chapter, we will cover pulling down strongholds. We read in Jeremiah 1:7-10

But the LORD said to me: "Do not say, 'I am a youth,' For you shall go to all to whom I send you, And whatever I command you, you shall speak.

Do not be afraid of their faces, for I am with you to deliver you," says the LORD. Then the LORD put forth His hand and touched my mouth, and the LORD said to me: "Behold, I have put My words in your mouth. See, I have this day set you over the nations and over the kingdoms, to root out and to pull down, to destroy and to throw down, to build and to plant." (NKJV)

Whenever we see a word in the Bible given by the Holy Spirit to a prophet, we should put ourselves in the place of the prophet, in that the Lord is actually speaking to us, to hear and do what the Lord could be teaching and saying. The Lord wants you to glean something from this passage. It is a principle found in this passage for us today. There are five things in this passage that we need to learn.

But first, let me remind you why this was written. It was written during the captivity of rebellious Israel and Judah who served other gods and because of that, they were being taken into captivity and brought as slaves into Babylon. It was a period of doom for the entire nation. At that time God raised up a prophet. His name was Jeremiah and his message was to warn the wicked and to comfort those who trusted in God. In the above passage God was placing him in that spiritual position to minister to the people in several ways. We can learn from those ways and apply them to spiritual warfare in today's times.

According to this passage God directed Jeremiah in spiritual warfare. These things were necessary to be done to utterly destroy and remove all the works of Satan in Israel. And so it is with us as well that these principles should be used in pulling down strongholds in our lives. First, Jeremiah had to ***root out*** (pluck up); second, he had to pull down or ***breakdown***, third, he had to ***destroy***, fourth, he had to **build**, and fifth, he had to **plant**.

Do you see this, after he plucked up and pulled down and destroyed and threw down (overthrow), he was instructed to build and to plant. It is our goal to follow this pattern of pulling down strongholds.

The devil takes advantage of every incident, every tragedy, everything that happens in a person's life, to take a control or attempt to take control of a person's life, and make a stronghold for himself in the imaginations of the mind. Now we have the right; the authority in Jesus' name, to root out, to pluck up, to pull down, destroy, and overthrow.

> *Behold, I give you the authority to trample on serpents and scorpions, and over all the power of the enemy, and nothing shall by any means hurt you.* Luke 10:19 (NKJV)

Right behind the tearing down and trampling the enemy, we have the Holy Spirit that comes along to plant and to build up.

So, Jesus gives us the right and the authority to root out or pluck up, to break down, to destroy, to overthrow all the power of the enemy. We have to constantly pull down the enemy's lies and strongholds that he builds up in our minds.

Some of these examples are, you're no good, you'll never be any good, you always fail, you are a born loser, you will never get a job, probably won't go to heaven, or something to this effect: I know it all, I'm smarter than other people, I'm pretty close to being perfect, I'm never wrong. You can't get rid of these problems when you accept the lies of Satan; they create strongholds in your mind.

One day, somebody said, "you're stupid," and what stuck in your head was: "You will never amount to anything in your life." Or, somebody said, "I don't want you," and you felt rejection from that point on, and rejection stuck in your thinking about yourself. Somebody said bad things to you or about you, and it stuck in your head and there it sits in your head today. These are lies from the enemy that are now stuck in your brain. But Jesus is more than a conqueror, and today we are going to pull down, pluck out, tear down and destroy what the enemy has placed in your head. **Say to yourself, "***stinking thinking; that is what it is***".**

The Lord says in Proverbs 23:7, *For as he thinks in his heart, so is he.* (NKJV) Family, if you think this way then that's the way you are and the devil has got your mind, and I know you don't want to be that way. Job said: *For the thing I greatly feared has come upon me, and what I dreaded has happened to me. Job 3:25* (NKJV)

Some of you have fear, a little fear, or a great fear, but guess what, whatever you fear is an open door and comes upon you. These are things that have been placed in your head by the lies of the enemy called strongholds. It is a constant war for control of your mind. There's a battle going on in your mind every day and whoever controls your mind, controls you. Every day you wake up there is a battle going on in your mind about what you think.

How do strongholds happen? How are they built in a person's mind? They are built by traumas, bad experiences, prejudices, because of the words, attitudes, or influence of others, sinful acts, justifying sin, bad habits, areas that have been repeatedly yielded to the enemy.

Some examples are, fears, depression, rejection, lust, anger, unbelief, hate, unforgiveness, bitterness, and many more. Strongholds are like a fort's being built, one brick at a time. One brick of wrong thinking upon another brick of wrong thinking until a fortress is built.

Who has strongholds? Everyone including Christians, everyone. What is a stronghold? It is an area of the mind set against God and His truth. It is an area of thinking that is set against righteousness and the principles of God. It can also be a network of lies by Satan that holds a person captive in unbelief, disobedience and sin. Strongholds can lodge within a person's soul which is composed of their thought life; (the mind, intellect, will and emotions.)

We are exposed to the philosophies of men, empty deceptions, prejudices, traditions of men and principles of the world every day of our lives, through friends, relatives, movies, books, TV, newspapers, magazines, computers, advertisements, schools, and people of influence.

Satan wants to control us, destroy our walk in Christ and our testimony of Jesus to others and to make our lives miserable and tormented. He deceives us into wrong thinking so that we harden our hearts and become incapable of knowing good from evil.

There are religions that war against flesh and blood; against people who do not believe the same way they believe. Christianity is at war against spiritual darkness, not against religions or people.

We know that Jesus is called the Prince of Peace, yes, that is His title, however in Matt. 10:34 Jesus said, *"Do not think that I came to bring peace upon the earth, I did not come to bring peace, but a sword."* Jesus came to bring a sword. Even though He is considered the Prince of Peace and walked as the Prince of Peace, He came to bring a sword. And He did war against one dark kingdom:

...for this purpose was the Son of God manifested, that He might destroy the works of the devil. 1 John 3:8 (NKJV)

Yes Jesus was a man of war, but it was not a war against flesh, but against spiritual forces.

For we do not wrestle against flesh and blood, but against principalities, against powers, against the rulers of the darkness of this age, against spiritual hosts of wickedness in the heavenly places. Eph. 6:12 (NKJV)

This is war, we are in a spiritual war. We struggle/wrestle against powers of darkness.

When we accept Jesus Christ as our personal Savior we enter the war. As soon as we say "I love you Jesus!"—Bam! We enter the spiritual war. From that day on we are in a war. It's a battle to the finish. It is not a bed of roses. It is an ugly war. But we know that we have the victory in Christ.

When Jesus died on the cross He said, "Telesti", "It is finished," which translated from Greek to English means, "Paid In Full." The punishment for all our sins, past, present and future, is Paid in Full.

Jesus finished his work on that cross, but our work is not finished yet. That is why He said to us, go lay hands on the sick and they will recover; go cast out demons in My name, Mark 16:17. His battle is finished but our part continues. We have good reasons to continue. In the book of Revelation:

Vs.2:7 To him who overcomes, ***I will grant to eat from the tree of life, which is in the Paradise of God. (NASB)***

Vs. 2:11 He who overcomes, ***will not be hurt by the second death.*** **(NKJV)**

Vs. 2:26 And he who overcomes, ***and he who keeps my deeds until the end, to him I will give authority over*** *nations.* **(NASB)**

Vs. 3:5 He who overcomes, *will be clothed in white garments and I will not blot out his name from the Book of Life; but I will confess his name before My Father and before His Angels.* **(NKJV)**

Vs. 3:12 He who overcomes, *I will make him a pillar in the temple of my God, and he shall go out no more. I will write on him the name of My God and the name of the city of My God, the New Jerusalem, which comes down out of heaven from My God. And I will write on him My new name.* **(NKJV)**

Vs. 21:7 He who overcomes, *shall inherit all things, and I will be his God and he shall be my son.* **(NKJV)**

These are good reasons to continue on in the war. Some may say that they're not strong enough to overcome; saying to themselves, "I've got problems. I just seemed to lose it from time to time. My heart thinks one way, but my mind thinks another and I just blow it!" Family, the Lord wants you to stay in the battle. Surrender yourself to His empowering presence, His grace, that will empower you to be all that He created you to be and to do all that He created you to do.

For whatever is born of God overcomes the world. And this is the victory that has overcome the world—our faith. Who is he who ***overcomes the world, but he who believes that Jesus is the Son of God?*** 1 John 5:4-5 (NKJV)

Family, it is our faith that keeps us pressed against the battle line. It is our faith in Jesus that overcomes the enemy. It is *this* war that we war to the end of life.

The pulling down of strongholds is essential to overcoming. Everyone has experienced anger and rage, but they are not the problem. Egotism intellectualism narcissism, addictions, impulses of all sorts are not the problem, they are symptoms of the problem. There is something beneath these things that cause the problems; *stinking thinking.* The problem is that there is a stronghold; a fortress in your mind. A fortress of darkness, dark thinking, selfish thinking, that blinds the truth from entering you and restrains the lie from leaving you.

This thing that we call a fortress, is a spiritual dark spot in your mind. The Apostle Paul tells us in 2 Corinthians 10:3-6

*For though we walk in the flesh, we do not war according to the flesh. For the weapons of our warfare are not carnal but **mighty in God** for pulling down strongholds, casting down arguments and every high thing that exalts itself against the knowledge of God, bringing every thought into captivity to the obedience of Christ, and being ready to punish all disobedience when your obedience is fulfilled.* (NKJV)

These weapons of war are mighty in God. I want you to think of an atomic bomb going off next to a building. In a flash the building would be gone. That is how powerful the weapons of our warfare are against the enemy. No matter how much steel or concrete that was there to support the structure, no matter how strong they build it, it would all dissolve and be gone. In a flash, it would become dust and rubble. **God has given us this type of mass destruction weapon against the strongholds in our mind. This makes you mighty men and women of war.**

Satan and his demons have been waging war against you for a long time, but when you come to realize that God has given you weapons for your warfare that are mighty in God for the destruction of fortresses in your mind, the war changes directions and you become victorious. You start to realize that you have these weapons. **The weapons are:** *the name of Jesus Christ, the blood of Jesus Christ* **and** *the*

word of your testimony-(which means--I testify to what God's Word declares for the situation I'm encountering).

Strongholds may exist in our minds, but they array themselves against us in our homes and private lives; they affect our spiritual and physical health. Often we are oppressed and give way to the enemy, instead of resisting and pulling down those strongholds.

In the Bible the apostle Paul tells us what God is doing through and because of the cross. He says in 1 Corinthians 1:19 *For it is written: "I will destroy the wisdom of the wise, And bring to nothing the understanding of the prudent."* (NKJV)

God is saying, there are some high and lofty thoughts that are about to come to an end. But to get the full impact of what He is saying to you, turn to the original quote from Isaiah 29:14-16:

> *Therefore, behold, I will again do a marvelous work among this people, a marvelous work and a wonder; for the wisdom of their wise men shall perish, and the understanding of their prudent men shall be hidden."*
>
> *Woe to those who seek deep to hide their counsel far from the LORD, and their works are in the dark; they say, "Who sees us?" and, "Who knows us?" Surely you have things turned around! Shall the potter be esteemed as the clay; for shall the thing made say of him who made it, "He did not make me"? Or shall the thing formed say of him who formed it, he has no understanding"?* (NKJV)

All these high and big thinking people; all their thoughts are vain. Why? Because they have no understanding, they are accusing God of getting it backwards. They consider themselves equal with God.

Sometimes big thinking can get us into trouble because it has darkness in it and it is in opposition to God. A lot of times we think we know better than God. Our minds are lofty and we think our thoughts are higher than God's thoughts. Sometimes we think that God has it all backwards and should be thinking the way we want Him to think. We have it all planned out and God is saying to us "What are you thinking?" "You've turned things around." Then we say to God, "No, You've turned things around. You don't see it the way it happened!"

Do you know why? Because our mind is twisted with darkness in it. We have beliefs that have been planted in our mind year after year over the course of our life due to incidents that occurred in our life which changed our way of thinking. We develop a pattern of thinking that is not of God. It is man's type of thinking filled with vain imagination. We believe that no one is watching; no one is taking account of what we say or do or how we act or what comes out of our mouth. My father used to say, "Whatever is in your heart will eventually come out of your mouth."

There is an opposition made against the gospel by the powers of sin and Satan. It is found in the very heart of man in his mind. Let's review 2 Corinthians 10:3-6 again:

3 For though we walk in the flesh, we do not war after the flesh: (For the weapons of our warfare are not carnal, but mighty through God to the pulling down of strong holds;)

4 Casting down imaginations, and every high thing that exalteth itself against the knowledge of God, and bringing into captivity every thought to the obedience of Christ;

5 And having in a readiness to revenge all disobedience, when your obedience is fulfilled. (KJV)

Verse 5 in the King James version uses the word "imaginations" not "arguments" as in some other translations. Arguments or imaginations are located in the minds of people. There is a supernatural battle going on where fortresses of darkness, those that are not made with flesh and blood, have held captive the minds of the saints, preventing *clear thinking, righteous thinking, holy thinking*. The King James Version calls this place in our minds, *"imaginations."* The New American Standard Bible calls this place in our minds *"speculations."* The New King James Version calls this place *"arguments."*

In researching for the correct word usage here in this passage, I looked up this passage in the <u>Interlinear Bible</u> which translates Greek directly into English and for this word they used ***imaginations*** - Strong's #3053. To get a clearer understanding of this passage I looked in Webster's dictionary and found the word imaginations was described as imaginary, existing only in the mind, unreal, fancied. Webster's dictionary described imagination as the power of the mind to form pictures, a mental image, or conception, creative mental power, creative images in the mind, full of fancies.

But in this passage in the Word of God, this is the place where our thinking is held captive. This is an imaginary place in our mind. This is place of mental pondering or reasoning that lifts itself up over the thinking of God. These are the areas that the apostle Paul writes to the Corinthian church that must be dealt with – imagination and man's thinking.

> This area is a place where men and women argue against God.

This place will restrict a Christian's growth. This is a place that holds lies that we have bought into and it keeps us in bondage. This is a place that makes us believe that a thing is, when it *really is not*.

> *O Jerusalem, wash your heart from wickedness that you may be saved. How long shall your evil thoughts lodge within you?* Jeremiah 4:14 (NKJV)

Paul also refers to this place in man that vain or wicked

thoughts lodge within a person. It is the seat of our minds; our imaginations.

> ^{14} *For we know that the law is spiritual, but I am carnal, sold under sin.* ^{15} *For what I am doing, I do not understand. For what I will to do, that I do not practice; but what I hate, that I do.* ^{16} *If, then, I do what I will not to do, I agree with the law that it is good.* ^{17} *But now, it is no longer I who do it, but sin that dwells in me.* ^{18} *For I know that in me (that is, in my flesh) nothing good dwells; for to will is present with me, but how to perform what is good I do not find.* ^{19} *For the good that I will to do, I do not do; but the evil I will not to do, that I practice.* ^{20} *Now if I do what I will not to do, it is no longer I who do it, but sin that dwells in me.* ^{21} *I find then a law, that evil is present with me, the one who wills to do good.* ^{22} *For I delight in the law of God according to the inward man.* ^{23} *But I see another law in my members, warring against the law of my mind, and bringing me into captivity to the law of sin which is in my members.* ^{24} *O wretched man that I am! Who will deliver me from this body of death?* ^{25} *I thank God— through Jesus Christ our Lord! So then, with the mind I myself serve the law of God, but with the flesh the law of sin.* Romans 7:14-25 (NKJV)

As you can see from this passage in verse 23 there is a law that brings us into captivity to the law of sin in our minds. This is a place of vain thinking and imaginations.

> *But solid food belongs to those who are of full age, that is, those who by reason of use have their senses exercised to discern both good and evil.* Hebrews 5:14 (NKJV)

This passage declares that those who are full of age or in another word, mature, who because of practice have their senses trained to discern good and evil. There is something going on with mature Christians. They are able to eat the solid food of the Word, and are able to discern good from evil, because they have practiced training their senses. Training means, exercising, firming it up.

> *Now may the God of peace Himself sanctify you completely; and may your whole spirit, soul, and body be preserved blameless at the coming of our Lord Jesus Christ.* 1 Thess. 5:23 (NKJV)

Preserve blameless – some of us leave out the body or soul or spirit in the sanctification process. We may say Lord, heal my body or we may say Lord, heal my spirit or we may say Lord, heal my soul, but we need to have all of it healed. Therefore we should say, "Lord, sanctify and purify my spirit, soul and body; please preserve my thought life and make it complete without blame." There is a process in cleaning out the old and bringing in the new. It is training your senses or training up your soul. Paul writes in Romans 12:1-2 (NKJV):

> *I beseech you therefore, brethren, by the mercies of God, that you present your bodies a living sacrifice, holy, acceptable to God, which is your reasonable service. And do not be conformed to this world, but be transformed by the renewing of your mind, that you may prove what is that good and acceptable and perfect will of God.*

Say to yourself, "Good-by stinking thinking. Hello renewed mind." Training up your senses is the process of renewing your mind and all aspects of Christ-like thinking. Thoughts that are good, thoughts that are acceptable, thoughts that are perfect, we need to train our minds to go in those directions.

If you tear down a stronghold or vain imagination and don't replace it with right or Christ-like thinking, you will be back to stinking thinking before you know it.

⁶ Be anxious for nothing, but in everything by prayer and supplication, with thanksgiving, let your requests be made known to God; ⁷ and the peace of God, which surpasses all understanding, will guard your hearts and minds through Christ Jesus.

⁸ Finally, brethren, whatever things are true, whatever things are noble, whatever things are just, whatever things are pure, whatever things are lovely, whatever things are of good report, if there is any virtue and if there is anything praiseworthy— meditate on these things. ⁹ The things which you learned and received and heard and saw in me, these do, and the God of peace will be with you. Philippians 4:6-9 (NKJV)

What did Paul say in verse 9? What you learned from me, what you received from me, what you heard from me, what you saw in me, do these things. In other words, practice what you saw in me. Paul was the example. If it worked for Paul, a formerly sinful man who persecuted Christians to the death, it will work for you.

Something may have happened in your life and you don't know what to do. You may say, my sister or my brother is doing this or that and it causes me distress or to stumble, or my friend said something and I'm really upset.

But what does God's Word say? Be anxious for nothing! But you reason to yourself, "You don't understand, if I don't do something or say something things are going to happen." Again, what does the scripture say? Be anxious for nothing. But you may say it's my nature to say this or that or to do something.

What does God's Word say? In Philippians 4:13 the Word says, *I can do all things through Christ who strengthens me.* But you may say "I'm afraid, if I do this, that I may fail." Do you remember what Job said in Job 22:28? *You will also declare a thing and it will be established for you so light will shine on your ways.* The opposite is also true. You may think or speak a dark, negative word and Satan and his demons will darken your path until it comes about.

Practice comparing what is in your mind to what God's Word says. Practice comparing your vain imaginations against God's truth. Hold Him (God) up as a litmus test to your thinking. There are a lot of imaginations happening in our minds; things that are unreal, concepts we have come to believe. There are mental pictures, that really didn't happen or won't happen, also arguments against God's ways. These mental pictures, speculations, vain imaginations, these thoughts become a fortress or a stronghold that hold our mind in captivity.

The Word of God tells us in 2 Corinthians 10:3-6 to cast down these imaginations and these thoughts that hold us captive and bring those thoughts into captivity. It is a process of not being held any longer to erroneous thoughts and being held captive by those thoughts but now we hold *them* captive to the obedience of Christ. As soon as you recognize that you are being held captive, say to yourself, "this is stinking thinking."

I've had to take my thoughts captive to obedience in the name of Jesus when evil thoughts enter my mind that are not good, that are not godly, that lead me down a road I don't want to go down. When I recognize this, I command it to be bound and powerless in the name of Jesus. I say to that spirit behind that thought, "You, the one that gives me this thought, I command you in the name of Jesus Christ to be bound in my mind. I command you to bow your knee before Jesus and to come out of my mind now. Leave my thoughts, leave my life now in the name of Jesus Christ.

It is at this point that I have completed 2 Cor.10: 3-5 and after that, I complete verse 6 by commanding all disobedience to obey by making my evil thoughts cease and bow their knee to Christ.

For God has not given us a spirit of fear, but of power and of love and of a sound mind. 2 Timothy 1:7 (NKJV)

The words "sound mind" used here actually means self-control in [Strong's 4995]. If your mind has the power for self-control through Jesus Christ, then you could hold your thoughts captive to the obedience of Christ.

Take look at the concept of a fence. A fence keeps things out and a fence keeps things in, and a self-controlled mind is like a fence. It is your responsibility to put up a fence for protection.

Deliverance from demons that have lodged themselves in our mind and thinking can be dislodged by doing a little soul searching. Let us ask the Holy Spirit to reveal to us truthfully what is in the recesses of our mind that is not of God.

Dear Heavenly Father, in the name of Jesus Christ, through the Holy Spirit, I ask that you reveal to us those hidden things that need to be rooted out, pulled down, destroyed, and thrown down. Oh Lord, show us what needs to be overthrown.

In Mark 16:17-18 You said, Lord Jesus *that these signs will follow those that believe. In my name they will cast out demons, they will speak with new tongues, they will take up serpents and if they drink anything deadly, it will by no means hurt them, they will lay hands on the sick, and they will recover.*

You said that these signs will follow those that believe. I believe you are the Son of the living God. I believe you came in the flesh. I believe you died on the cross. I believe you shed your blood for me. I believe you died and rose again. I believe that you are God in the flesh, to give me eternal life, and save my soul from eternal damnation, to destroy the

works of the devil in me and around me so that I might have life and life abundantly.

As a believer with signs following me, I cast out demons that are present in my life that are present in my mind, and my imagination, and my thinking, and my flesh.

Now, address these spirits aloud:

I therefore in Jesus' name command out of me and away from me every evil spirit of:

Oppression, opposition, condemnation, compromise, egotism, intellectualism, self-love, false compassion, false humility, insecurity, inferiority, low self-esteem, pride, spirits that make me brag, mockery, judging, accusations, false prophet, false witness, sexual perversion, masturbation, lust, fantasy lust, immorality, curse of the bastard, gigolo, anger, fear, materialism, rejection, rebellion, confusion, addiction, sorcery, rage, sickness, spirits of infirmity, mental illness,

I command these evil spirits to go and all kindred spirits to leave me now in the name of Jesus Christ. Now take a deep breath and blow out breath. Go, in the name of Jesus Christ.

In the name of Jesus Christ, I command out of me all spirits of:

Discontent, lying to self, cover-up lies, cringing fear, fear of failure, dishonor to self, dishonor of others, futility, foolish reasoning, false speculations, false assumptions, stupid speculations, senseless mind, foolishness, lack of knowledge, lack of wisdom, sexual idolatry, impurity, homosexuality, bisexuality, lesbianism, indecency, incest, loathsomeness, unrighteousness, iniquity, guilt, covetousness, grasping, greed, malice, envy, jealousy, murder, strife, deceit, treachery, ill will, cruel ways, backbiting, gossip.

I command these evil spirits to go and all kindred spirits to leave me now in the name of Jesus Christ. Take a deep breath and blow out. Go, in Jesus' name.

In the name of Jesus Christ, I command out of me all spirits of; Slander, hating God, insolence, arrogance, boasting, inventor of evil, rebellion against parents, having no understanding, without conscience, faithlessness, heartlessness, loneliness, mercilessness, fantasy, poverty in soul, poverty in spirit, poverty in body, poverty in pocket book, want, lack, insufficiency, rationalization, murmuring and complaining, pride, scoffer, arrogant, ungrateful, boasters, bragging, unholy, profane, callous, inhumane, hardhearted, relentless, unforgiving, lacking natural affections, troublemaker, false accuser, loose morals, fierce, hater of good, treacherous, betrayer, disloyalty, rashness, hypocrisy, vain amusements, vain imaginations, ingratitude.

I command these evil spirits to go and all kindred spirits to leave me now in the name of Jesus Christ. Take a deep breath and blow out. Go, in Jesus' name.

The following portion of deliverance on SELF is taken from the Deliverance Manual written by Gene B. Moody pages 303 & 304.

In the name of Jesus Christ, I command out of me the following spirits of Self:

Self-abhorring, self-absorbed, self-abused, self-accusation, self- admiring, self- annihilation, self-appointed, self-assumed, self- awareness, self-banished, self-betrayal, self-blinded, self-centered, self-collected, self-conceited, self-condemnation, self- conflict, self-conscious, self-consuming, self-contained, self-contempt, self-contradiction, self-criticism, self-crucifixion, self-deceiving, self- deception, self- degrading, self-deluded, self-delusion, self- depraved, self-depreciation, self-despair, self-destroying, self- distraction, self-devouring, self-display, self-distrust, self esteem.

I command these evil spirits to go and all kindred spirits to leave me now in the name of Jesus Christ. Take a deep breath and blow out. Go, in Jesus' name.

In the name of Jesus Christ, I command out of me all following **spirits of Self:**

Self-exaggeration, self-exalting, self-exposure, self-flattery, self- forgetfulness, self- hatred, self-harming, self-good, self-idolized, self-ignorant, self-importance, self-indignation, self-indulging, self-affliction, self-interest, selfishness, self-killed, self- destroying, self-loathing, self-loving, self-made, self-neglecting, self-oblivion, self-opinionated, self-pity, self-pleasing, self- preference, self-pride, self-reproving, self- repulsive, self- restriction, self-resident, self-reference, self-righteousness, self- received, self-scorn, a self-seduction, self-seeking, self-starved, self-suppression, self-suspicious, self-tormenting, self-torture, self- unforgiveness, self-willed, self-worshiper, self-wronged.

I command these evil spirits to go and all kindred spirits to leave me now in the name of Jesus Christ. Take a deep breath and blow out. Go, in Jesus' name.

Prayer to the Holy Spirit:

Come Holy Spirit, Come Lord Jesus, I ask that you come into these areas that were just swept clean and take up residence. I now give You these areas where demons had control over my life and I surrender these areas to You, to rule and reign in. Be Lord of my life. I give these areas to You and I surrender them to You for Your Lordship. Amen.

Chapter 6
Emotional Triggers

For God has not given us a spirit of fear, but of power and of love and of a sound mind. 2 Timothy 1:7 (NKJV)

In this passage, Paul reminds Timothy and us that God does not give us a spirit of fear. Fear is an emotion and we can see also from this passage that a spirit can attach itself to one of our emotions; the emotion of fear.

"Be angry, and do not sin; do not let the sun go down on your wrath, nor give place to the devil. Ephesians 4:26-27 (NKJV)

We see in this scripture that it is OK to be angry, but not to take anger to bed with us, for if we don't come to peace about the situation, then it gives a place for the devil to work inside of us. When we give a place for anger to dwell in us, that is where the devil attaches evil spirits to work anger into unforgiveness and bitterness and retaliation and other emotional responses. Evil spirits can attach them selves to our emotions and intensify those emotions and trigger other emotions.

(Some material in this chapter is taken from a cassette tape entitled "Deactivating Our Emotional Triggers" tape 1 of 3 by Dr. Gary Greenwald)

All of us have emotional triggers, some are beneficial to us and some are harmful to us. Triggers are response patterns to our memories. In everyone's life there are certain words when said, trigger emotions. There is an old saying, "that person knows how to push my buttons." It is used to express that the person knows how to trigger an emotion by using words.

But in every one of us there are feelings that can be triggered and they can set off an emotional response. This is where I believe the enemy would want to operate. If he can make us look bad by having a bad emotional response to something, it discredits our Christianity, thus giving Christ a bad name.

We all have emotional triggers that cause us to do things that we did not expect to do. We all seem to have self-defeating, self- sabotaging triggers that operate in our lives Have you ever been taken over by a flood of emotions that cause you to do and say things that you later regretted and "fly off the handle" and "lose it?"

It might have manifested as a temporary outburst that made you feel like you just wanted to throw something at somebody, or you are repulsed and rejected by someone and you don't know why they repulsed you, but you just want to get away from them and reject them, or you find that you are falling into a loathsome habit, you hate the habit, you repent and fall right back into it again by something that triggers it.

Something triggers us emotionally and for a period of time, we seem out of control. This reminds me of the scripture apostle Paul writes to us in Romans 7:19-25:

> *For the good that I want, I do not do, but I practice the very evil that I do not want. But if I am doing the very thing I do not want, I am no longer the one doing it, but sin which dwells in me. I find then the principle that evil is present in me, the one who wants to do good. For I joyfully concur with the law of God in the inner man, but I see a different law in the members of my body, waging war against the law of my mind and making me a prisoner of the law of sin which is in my members. Wretched man that I am! Who will set me free from the body of this death? Thanks be to God through Jesus Christ our Lord! So then, on the one hand I myself with my mind am serving the law of God, but on the other,*

with my flesh the law of sin. (NASB)

Family, we all want to follow and produce the fruits of the Holy Spirit, Love, Joy, Peace, Patience, Kindness, Goodness, Faithfulness, Gentleness, Self–control (Gal 5:22). But then, someone does or says something and that triggers an emotion and we do the things we don't want to do, or we say the thing we didn't want to say and we lose control of our emotions. Have you ever done that?

2 Cor. 10:3-6 speaks to us about strongholds or fortresses in our mind. The mind is the soul of man and it consists of intellect, will and emotions. When words or actions trigger unhealthy and destructive emotions in us, or threatens us, it may be because there are ungodly **strongholds of the enemy that are set up in our minds that control us.**

We saw how important 2 Cor. 10:3-6 was in the previous Chapter, but let's look it over again in regard to emotional triggers, using the New American Standard Bible translation.

*For though we walk in the flesh, we do not war according to the flesh, for the weapons of our warfare are not of the flesh, but divinely powerful for the destruction of fortresses. (strongholds) We are destroying speculations (imaginations) and every lofty thing raised up against the knowledge of God, and we are taking every thought captive to the obedience of Christ, and we are ready to **punish all disobedience**, whenever your obedience is complete.* 2 Corinthians 10:3-6 (NASB)

1. We don't win the war according to the flesh, with fleshly will- power or resistance, or fortitude, or inner strength. We cannot fight thoughts in our minds with fleshly warfare.

2. The weapons that we use to fight the fight in our thought

life are **divinely powerful**. In other words, they come from a supernatural source. Zechariah 4:6 tells us, *"Not by **might** nor by **power**, but by my **Spirit**," says the LORD Almighty.*

3. Verse 6 declares that we are ready to punish all disobedience. The problem is that most of us are not taking control of our emotions, and reactions *(**not punishing**, **our emotional disobedience, our emotional feelings, our emotional reactions**).* This means that we accomplish the solution to our carnal problems by controlling and taking them captive and submitting them to the Lord Jesus Christ.

Wouldn't our lives be far better if *we* were in control of our lives *through Christ* instead of being controlled by some emotional outburst or negative action caused by a negative emotion? Here is the good news – these emotional strongholds must be deactivated and dismantled by the Holy Spirit and then they can be pulled down by God's Spirit and only by God's Spirit. Our weapons are mighty through God for overcoming these self-defeating, self- sabotaging trigger *mechanisms.*

We emotionally react when something is said or done to us and we associate it with something that was said or done to us in the past. Something that was said or done today reminds us of something that was done in the past. Now in that association we subconsciously think that the past event is being repeated today, so we respond and over-react to the situation.

Example:

You grew up in a home with a father or a mother who physically or emotionally abused you and they wouldn't listen to anything you had to say and you were severally punished for things you didn't do. You grew to hate them for not listening and unjustly punishing you. So when you grew up and had a family of your own the slightest argument would escalate into a shouting match because your spouse would not listen to your side of the argument and that pushed "*your button*" because it reminded you of something that was done to you in the past that wounded you.

Now every disagreement in the present makes you think it is happening to you all over again. And all that burning anger that was associated to your abusive parent is now directed to your spouse. There are probably millions of marriages that are on the rocks because they haven't dealt with the triggers that remind them of past experiences.

There are several ways that can bring about emotional responses that were triggered by words or actions. One way is through traumas, verbal or physical abuse, rape, beatings, molestation, trapped in a freezer or under water, buried alive or caught in a fire. These things are recorded in your memory never to be forgotten. They are written in your mind like with a permanent marker.

Another way for emotion triggers to affect you is when something that has happened to you repeatedly your whole life continues to be happening. There is an unconscious response, like a knee jerk reaction when the doctor tests your reflexes with the little rubber hammer.

When these triggering mechanisms are operating, you may try to control your emotions, attitudes and responses for years, but because they are unconscious reactions, you don't seem to have control over them.

The Bible says in Prov. 25:28: *He that hath no rule over his own spirit is like a city that is broken down, and without walls.* (KJV) When a person can't rule his own human spirit and his own emotions, then his walls as the Bible says, are "broken down." That condition means that you have become open for the enemy to come in with physical, emotional and spiritual illnesses. To have the abundant life that Jesus promised in John 10:10, we must destroy the triggers that set off our harmful emotions.

Memory recall can bring us joy as we remember the good things about people and places, but the enemy of our soul will use memory recall to set us on a course to destroy us. We will deal with this spiritually at the end of this lesson.

Our mind works in mysterious ways. When we have done something that is wrong in the past, we naturally feel guilty and a feeling that punishment is on the way. And when something triggers that guilt today, you feel that you should be punished for past wrong doings.

Guilt and shame set a person's mind on the road to depression which causes the mind to make wrong choices, sometime to the point of becoming accident prone in order to punish oneself because of underlying feelings of unworthiness. Shame and guilt also affects the immune system to make one sick. The Bible tells us His Word will be health to all our flesh in Prov. 4:20 -23:

*My son, attend to my words; incline thine ear unto my sayings. Let them not depart from thine eyes; keep them in the **midst of thine heart**, for they are **life** unto those that find them, and **health** to all their flesh. **Keep thy heart with all diligence**; for out of it are the issues of life.* (KJV)

The Word of God is real truth and cancels the lie of the enemy. When we believe His words then His words become health to all our flesh. This scripture is powerfully related to Paul's words in 2 Corinthians 10:3-5:

For though we walk in the flesh, we do not war according to the flesh, for the weapons of our warfare are not of the flesh, but divinely powerful for the destruction of fortresses. We are destroying speculations and every lofty thing raised up against the knowledge of God, and we are taking every thought

captive to the obedience of Christ…
Examples of how triggers work in our lives

1. Our mind connects traumas or emotional events together with a connecting link or trigger. Sometimes these triggers are words, objects, or events that produce an involuntary emotional response.

An example. There was a woman who years ago was driving her car and ran a red light and caused an accident. Just before impact, the other vehicle blasted its horn and then came the impact. From that moment on, any time she hears the blasting of a car horn she reacts as if the event is happening again and she begins to panic and become terrified and shout out to her husband who is driving in present time "What did you do wrong to make them mad at you?" She immediately assigns blame to her husband who is driving the vehicle that she is now in because of what happened to her in her past accident. In her accident, she was at fault.

In the present time, her husband is innocent. It was two other drivers honking at each other, but she blames her husband for her fear because her emotions have been triggered by a car horn. She may experience fear and anger every time she is out in traffic and hears a car horn and then feels she must place blame for her emotional distress. <u>The stronghold in her mind is an imagination</u> <u>triggered by the sound of a car horn.</u>

As I stated in the previous Chapter, 2 Cor. 10:3-6 says that this is an imagination that must be dismantled and cast down and made captive to the obedience of Jesus Christ. In other words, these thoughts must be made to submit to Christ by claiming that the sound of a loud horn is symbolizing a horrible accident is about to occur. This is a lie of the enemy in her mind. Satan is the father of lies. (John 8:44). And she must command these lying thoughts to come to obedience to the Lord.

Any time a person wants to dismantle something, they look for the places where connections are and undue the bolts and the nuts in that location. Once that is done, the structure collapses more easily.

The stronghold in her mind was an imagination. That imagination sets up an opinion, pretense, thought. These opinions and thoughts are not only hostile towards God, but they are hostile against you and your abundant life. These are reflections of memories that determine conduct.

Another Example: A woman came to me for help. She had a fear of particular words. After digging into her life history, I found that when she was younger she had overheard her father and mother speaking privately about how they loved her brother more than her. She was never the same after that. Her mind associated rejection with punishment and the Lake of Fire mentioned in Revelation 20:14-15. Any time she heard her father's name or heard or saw the word *lake* of any word that sounded like lake, she would flip out into great fear with screaming and crying. This brought attention to her. I believe that is what satisfied and appeased the demon that was controlling her (negative attention). The evil spirit in her convinced her that any attention was better than rejection. So now she associated trigger words such as her father's name, lake, or any word that sounded like lake such as ache, snake, bake, Jake, and fire or eternal, with the feeling of rejection.

Since her spirit was wounded and crushed by the words of her father and she loved her father, but inside she felt that he was lost and he would be punished in the Lake of Fire for wounding her. Now when she heard or saw those particular words she would react out of protection for her father so he wouldn't be thrown in the Lake of fire. Religiosity turned into religious O.C.D. or better known as

"Scrupulosity," that is Religious Obsessions or Religious Compulsions." Her whole destructive emotional life is now triggered by words from a conversation that she overheard when she was young and impressionable.

She refused to be set free because this religious fear was now her controlling factor and negative attention was now what she strived for. Some people do not really wish to be healed even though they say so.

Jesus found a man at the pool of Bethesda who was waiting for the stirring of the healing water. When Jesus saw him lying there, and knew that he already had been *in that condition* a long time, He said to him in John:5:6, "Do you want to be made well?"

Some people who are in terrible conditions sometimes do not really want to be made well even though they position themselves for it. They have another motive for remaining ill, such as controlling others, taking solace in a pity party or forcing others to take care of them or pay attention to them as I mentioned above.

2. A second way triggers work is when something consistently happens to you-- your whole life.

Do you all remember Pavlov's dog? Pavlov developed an experiment where he took a dog and when he would ring a bell, he would feed the dog. After a period of time he noticed that the dog would salivate during the ringing of the bell. He eventually rang the bell with out feeding the dog and the dog continued to salivate even without being fed. The two stimuli, bell and food were linked together in a repeated pattern. The dog knew that when he heard the bell, that he was about to get food so he salivated.

People seem to re-act the same way too. Let's say you had an abusive parent and they constantly put you down, mocking you, calling you names or making you feel stupid and in the process they point a finger at you or put their hands on their hip or some other action while they are putting you down.

You associate their action with the put down. Years later after you have grown up you may be in conversation with someone and they disagree with you and in the process of their disagreeing with you they do the same gestures that your parent did when they put you down. Immediately something rises up in you and you get emotional and blow up at them. Anger and rage rise up in you and you lose it and blow your stack at them and go way over the top. You associate it with the put down of your abusive parent and it was sparked by the gestures or movements of the person whom you are presently disagreeing with. This is called conditioned response just like Pavlov's dog.

Wouldn't it be better for everyone if you are in control of your own emotions? Proverbs 16:32 says *He who is slow to anger is better than the mighty, and he who rules his spirit than he who takes a city.* (NKJV)

If you are in control of your own spirit then you won't be easily be triggered into ungodly emotions:

Take heed, watch and pray; for you do not know when the time is. It is like a man going to a far country, who left his house and gave authority to his servants, and to each his work, and commanded the doorkeeper to watch. Watch therefore, for you do not know when the master of the house is coming—in the evening, at midnight, at the crowing of the rooster, or in the morning— lest, coming suddenly, he find you sleeping. And what I say to you, I say to all: Watch!" Mark 13:33-40 (NKJV)

As you can see this scripture works outside of our lives and for the work of building the kingdom externally and it also works inside each individual to the guarding and watching of what is inside the house as well. In this scripture we are charged to watch and guard what is going on inside of us. We are to learn how to **guard and protect our senses and emotions,** because throughout life, we have unconsciously dropped things into our brains that are destructive to us.

The work of guarding the kingdom of God which is within us is very necessary for the advancement of Kingdom of God outside of us. We read in Luke 17:20-21 (NKJV)

> *Now when He was asked by the Pharisees when the kingdom of God would come, He answered them and said, "The kingdom of God does not come with observation; nor will they say, 'See here!' or 'See there!' For indeed, the kingdom of God is <u>**within you**</u>."*

Some translations say **"is in your midst"** but the actual word means <u>***within you***</u>**."** (Greek word is Evtos), (Strong's #1787). *For the Kingdom of God is **within you**.*

We must guard the Kingdom of God that is within us as Philippians 4:6-7 instructs us:

> *Do not be anxious about anything, but in everything**, by prayer and petition,** with thanksgiving, present your requests to God. And the peace of God, which transcends all understanding, **will guard your hearts and your minds in Christ Jesus.*** (NIV)

Proverbs 4:23 confirms this: *"Above all else, guard your heart, for it is the wellspring of life."*

The work of dismantling emotional triggers that have been set up in the kingdom that is within ourselves, which God has asked us to guard and protect, is by the Holy Spirit, who we have received; through the gifts of the Holy Spirit – the discerning of the Holy Spirit, the

word of knowledge by the Holy Spirit, prophecy by the Holy Spirit.

Here is a caution that everyone should hear. If we don't allow God's Spirit to release us eventually it will even cause our immune system to be affected we will begin to break down. It takes a lot of energy to hold down subconscious wounds and hurts and to try to subdue those from coming up and exploding as if we are walking volcanoes.

Many are held captive to triggers simply because they do not fully understand the depth of 2 Tim 1:7 where God speaks to us about our mind (soul). *For God hath not given us the spirit of fear;*
but of power, and of love, and of a sound mind. (KJV)

The word for **fear** in Greek according to Strong's concordance #1167. deilia *di-lee'-ah* from #1169; timidity – fear. deilos *di-los'* from deos (dread); timid, i.e. (by implication) **faithless:--fearful.** It is a **cowardice type fear.**

And the Greek word for sound mind is Strong's #4995. sophronismos *so-fron-is-mos'* from 4994; discipline, i.e. self- control:--sound mind.

There is a spirit that is constantly trying to undermine a part of our mind. There are Christians that have **great love** and **great power** that part of their mind operates in their salvation, but a **sound mind**, a **disciplined mind**, a **self controlled mind** eludes them. This part of their mind does not operate in the way it should through the saving grace of Jesus. They seem to have no power to hold thoughts captive to the obedience of Christ.

Our mind is our soul and the bible speaks to the condition of our soul over 1500 times in the Bible. This must be very important if it is dealt with over 1500 times in The Word. God wants our soul with its thoughts and actions to conform to the image of Jesus Christ.

For whom He foreknew, He also predestined to **be conformed to the image of His Son**, *that He might be the firstborn among many brethren.* Romans 8:29 (NKJV)

that you put off, concerning your former conduct, the old man which grows corrupt according to the deceitful lusts, and be **renewed in the spirit of your mind,** *and that you put on the new man which was created according to God, in true righteousness and holiness.* Ephesians 4:22-24 (NKJV)

I beseech you therefore, brethren, by the mercies of God, that you present your bodies a **living sacrifice**, *holy, acceptable to God, which is your reasonable service. And do not be conformed to this world, but be transformed by the* **renewing of your mind**, *that you may prove what is that good and acceptable and perfect will of God.* Romans 12:1-2 (NKJV)

You see, if you don't let God have control and renew your mind then your character will never produce the fruit of the Holy Spirit. You will have some rotten character faults.

The key to healing your emotions is to learn where you were hurt in the past. When depression, escape, anger, jealousy, arguments, strife, arise in your life today, the key to stopping these things dead in their tracks and for healing to begin is to go back to your life's history, asking the Holy Spirit the questions, " Why am I feeling this today? What is the real reason behind this emotion?" And you will see the Holy Spirit bringing you back to the source of your emotion.

I have done this many times in the middle of an emotion. I stop and ask the Holy Spirit why I am feeling this absurd way and many times he brings to remembrance some childhood experience and that then brings me to my knees and I understand as He brings it all out into the open for healing. Then I ask for forgiveness for my negative emotion.

Family, is there anything that is haunting you from the past? Any secret sin that you did or was done to you and you have tucked it down and swept it under the carpet? The devil will attempt to make that a stronghold in your mind and anything that reminds you of it is a trigger to make you crumble and cave in on that emotion.

Healing begins when you pronounce forgiveness. Everything is under the blood of Jesus Christ. He has forgiven you. The true body of Christ has forgiven you. But you must forgive yourself. You see family; the only one who is reminding you of it, is the accuser of the brethren—Satan.

God does not want you to live out a defeated life style

. We must believe in the power of God and live as if Jesus lives inside of us and manifests Himself inside our bodies.

But we have this treasure in earthen vessels, that the excellence of the power may be of God and not of us. We are hard-pressed on every side, yet not crushed; we are perplexed, but not in despair; persecuted, but not forsaken; struck down, but not destroyed— always carrying about in the body the dying of the Lord Jesus, that the life of Jesus also may be manifested in our body. 2 Corinthians 4:7-10 (NKJV)

But we all, with open face beholding as in a glass the glory of the Lord, are changed into the same image from glory to glory, even as by the Spirit of the Lord. 2 Corinthians 3:18 (KJV)

I want God's Spirit to change me into his image. If I have character faults and patterns of reactions, I want those to be brought under the blood of Jesus. It is an exhausting experience to have to battle these things over and over again, so the object is to get to the root of it once and for all.

We must let the Holy Spirit expose our triggers because we **don't** want to continue in our habitual thought patterns, and our reactionary patterns because **they develop** into rotten attitudes that are pessimistic, negative, judgmental, or critical, and these attitudes didn't happen overnight but were formed by patterns. You became that way over many years.

Here is how we will co-operate with the Holy Spirit to change us into God's image.

Proverbs 20:27 *The spirit of man is the lamp of the LORD, Searching all the innermost parts of his being.* (NASB)

Another way to say this is:

God will use our human spirit as his flashlight to search the innermost parts and secrets of our lives. He will use our spirit as a lamp and go into those places that are hidden.

But he who is joined to the Lord is one spirit with Him. 1 Cor.6:17. So our human spirit is already united with the God's Holy Spirit and the two will work together. We are co-laborers with the Holy Spirit in the searching out process. *For what man knows the things of a man accept the spirit of the man which is in him?* 1 Corinthians 2:11 (NKJV)

This implies that our human spirit joined with the Holy Spirit knows all the subconscious and unconscious levels of our memories. Right now, let us let the Holy Spirit deal with those things He surfaces in us and only those issues.

Prayer:
> Dear Heavenly Father, according to Proverbs 20:27 (NASB), the spirit of man is the lamp of the LORD, searching all the innermost parts of his being. Your word also declares in 1 Cor. 6:17, that the one who is joined to the Lord is one spirit *with Him*. So I claim that my human spirit and the Holy Spirit are joined together as one in searching out the hidden things in my life.
>
> I join in with you O Lord, and ask you, Lord, to search me and expose what needs to be dealt with in Jesus' name. Show me the truth of what may have happened in that event where there was hurt, where there was abuse, in situations that happened over and over and over again, and what the link and connections to those situations and mechanisms might be, that triggers me off. Show me what traumatic event that might have happened that has caused me to be like this in this point of my life--to not be able to give myself in a real committed relationship.
>
> Expose those things that cause me to erupt like a geyser or go into rage or isolation every time certain words are spoken, or certain pictures form in my mind. Father, help me to see what the trigger is, that has caused me not to be balanced and emotionally stable, in Jesus' name.

I am going to mention certain emotional categories or root causes and I want you to write down whatever comes to your mind, that is, if you have specific reactions to these root causes. I not looking for an emotional response, but I am looking for something that is being brought back to your memory. So when one of these roots applies to your life, jot it down.

Write down what name, picture, scene, incident or event, or memory comes to your mind when I call these things out. Whether they were **one time** incidents or **repetitive** incidents make a note of it. Let the Holy Spirit and you flush these out so that we can pull them down in Jesus' name.

Pray aloud the following prayer:

I bind every evil spirit that has set up a stronghold in my mind and bind them in Jesus' name. I bind every evil spirit that has attached itself to an emotional trigger in my life, that controls me and keeps me bound. I sever the link between the stimuli and those inner emotional drives, those unconscious reactions that are ungodly, and I sever these links in the name of Jesus.

Father, I ask you in the name of Jesus Christ to reveal to me all demonic, emotional triggers that make me react in an ungodly way and the things responsible for those triggers and the demons behind them. I ask you to bring them to my mind so that they may be dealt with.

I take authority in the name of Jesus Christ and shatter all emotional triggers of the enemy and command spirits of them out of me in the name of Jesus. I now pull down out of my mind and command destroyed all demonic mental images, every trigger, every demon behind those triggers in Jesus' name.

Now I am just going to name them and when it strikes something in you, I want you to circle the word and write the word down and any thought or mental picture that goes with it that affects you or sounds like your issue.

As you go through the steps of deliverance, when you renounce and command out the evil spirits, <u>speak out loud</u>

In Jesus' name, I command out of me the triggers and the spirits of these triggers:

Rejection, abandonment, failure, negativity, pessimism, judgmentalism, opposition, condemnation, guilt, criticism, betrayal, fear of commitment, fear of responsibility, fear of authority, fear of diseases, fear of darkness, fear of being alone, fear of death, fear of being closed in, fear of a sound, fear of foods, fear of stimuli....Name your own fear....In the name of Jesus, I take authority over these emotional triggers over the emotional stimuli over all *workings* and *mechanisms* that connect them to each other, over all mental images, over every trigger and every demon behind these triggers now in Jesus' name. Take a deep breath and blow out. Go! In Jesus' name.

<u>Write down</u> what came to your mind just then – a person, place or incident, a picture of something in your mind.

Now I command out of me every emotional trigger and mechanism that ties them together in Jesus' name. Go in Jesus' name. (Blow out breath). Leave in Jesus' name!

In Jesus' name, I command out of me the triggers and the spirits of these triggers:

Punishment, discontentment, dishonor to self, to others, fear of losing honor, fear of being punished, hopelessness, helplessness, humiliation, put downs, ridicule, failure, stupid thinking, stupid decisions, senseless mind, foolishness, lack of knowledge, lack of wisdom. In the name of Jesus,

I take authority over these emotional triggers, over the emotional stimuli, over all *gears* and *mechanisms* that connect them to each other, over all mental images, over every trigger and every demon behind these triggers now in Jesus name. Take a deep breath and blow out. Go! In Jesus' name.

Write down what came to your mind just then – a person, place or incident, a picture of something in your mind.

Now I command out of me every emotional trigger and mechanism that ties them together in Jesus' name. Go in Jesus' name. [Blow out breath]. Leave in Jesus' name!

In Jesus name, I command out of me the triggers and the spirits of these triggers:

Sexual idolatry, homosexuality, greed, troubled heart, poverty of spirit, poverty of soul, poverty of the body, lack, insufficiency, pride, trouble receiving, trouble maker, attention seeking, callousness, hard-hearted, cruelty, revengeful, cold love, cold shoulder, punishing others, ungrateful, false front, denial, stealing, lying, dishonesty, stretching the truth, craftiness, schemer, always controlling and maneuvering others.

In the name of Jesus, I take authority over these emotional triggers, over the emotional stimuli, over all *gears* and *mechanisms* that connect them to each other, over all mental images, over every trigger and every demon behind these triggers now in Jesus' name. Take a deep breath and blow out. Go! In Jesus' name.

Now write down what came to your mind just then – a person, place or incident, a picture of something in your mind.

Now I command out of me every emotional trigger and mechanism that ties them together in Jesus' name. Go in Jesus' name [Blow out breath]. Leave in Jesus' name!

In Jesus' name, I command out of me the triggers and the spirits of these triggers:

Rudeness, traitor, cowardice, turmoil, muddled mind, forgetfulness, superiority, depression, flashbacks, painful thoughts, escape, hysteria, losing control, withdrawal, nervousness, loss of concentration, sloppiness, temper, irritation, hostility, bitter love, self-centeredness.

In the name of Jesus, I take authority over these emotional triggers over the emotional stimuli, over all *gears* and *mechanisms* that connect them to each other, over all mental images, over every trigger and every demon behind these triggers now in Jesus name. Take a deep breath and blow out. Go! In Jesus name.

Now write down what came to you mind just then – a person, place or incident, a picture of something in your mind. Now I command out of me every emotional trigger and mechanism that ties them together in Jesus' name. Go in Jesus' name. (Blow out breath). Leave in Jesus' name!

In Jesus' name, I command out of me the triggers and the spirits of these triggers:

Addiction, addictiveness, bad habits, ungodly compulsions and cravings, slavery or bondage to sin, procrastination, nervousness, stress, tension, distrust, unreliability, fear of looking stupid, self- hate for wrong decisions, abuse, self-abuse, emotional abuse, mental abuse, physical abuse, sexual abuse, anger.

In the name of Jesus, I take authority over these emotional triggers, over the emotional stimuli, over all *gears* and *mechanisms* that connect them to each other, over all mental images, over every trigger and every demon behind these triggers now in Jesus' name. Take a deep breath and blow out. Go! In Jesus' name.

Now **write down** what came to your mind just then – a person, place or incident, a picture of something in your mind. Now I command out of me every emotional trigger and mechanism that ties them together in Jesus' name. Go in Jesus' name. (Blow out breath). Leave in Jesus' name!

In Jesus name, I command out of me the triggers and the spirits of these triggers

Guilt, rage, out of control anger**,** pain, sickness, compromise, intellectualism, egotism, bragging, pride, automatic response, accident prone, self-destruction.

In the name of Jesus, I take authority over these emotional triggers, over the emotional stimuli, over all *gears* and *mechanisms* that connect them to each other, over all mental images, over every trigger and every demon behind these triggers now in Jesus' name. Take a deep breath and blow out. Go! In Jesus' name.

Now **write down** what came to your mind just then – a person, place or incident, a picture of something in your mind. Now I command out of me every emotional trigger and mechanism that ties them together in Jesus' name. Go in Jesus' name. (Blow out breath). Leave in Jesus' Name!

In Jesus' name, I command out of me the triggers and the spirits of these triggers:

Self-destructing negative inner vows, such as "I will never let anyone do(name whatever vow you made)... to me again." Maybe it was a domineering mother, father, husband, wife, so you close all input from outside sources. **Inner vows** start with: "I will never let" and usually ends with "to me ever again." I will never be dominated by a woman again, I will never be dominated by a man again. So you will not listen to a man again or a woman again for any input. I will never trust a man again, I will never let anyone touch me again. I will never do that. I will never be poor again. I will never let anyone tell me what to do again. I will never have children. I will never get married. I will never sit under a woman pastor.

Or they can sound like this: I'm so stupid, I'm not smart enough, I'm not strong enough, I'm too weak, I'm not confident enough." I'm too old, I'm tone deaf, I can't sing. I'm too sick, I can't dance, I can't swim, I can't draw, I don't have the talent. I'll never be happy again, I can't pay my bills. These are inner vows that can cause you to shut down in certain areas of your lives. If this applies to you **write down** these inner vows.

Some have been conditioned to believe you cannot be spiritual if you have nice things. We have been conditioned to believe that we have to be poor in order to be spiritual. This is a lie.

In Jesus' name I break the following lies about:

Money squeamishness, anti-success, anti-prosperity, fear of success, religious spirit, false spirituality about money, a spirit that makes me believe that I should have no money, no comforts, few material things, because I have been conditioned to believe I can not be spiritual if I have nice things, I break and sever the words I spoke against myself in self-imposed curses when I made these inner vows, and I command them to be void of their power over me, over my life, and over my future in the name of Jesus Christ and I now command every and all demons who were assigned to these inner vow curses to leave their assignments and leave me now in Jesus' name. Take a deep breath and blow it out. Go in Jesus' name!

Now write down what came to your mind just then – a person, place or incident, a picture of something in your mind. Hold them up over your head and proclaim, self-imposed inner vow curses, your power be broken and the emotional triggers that came by you leave me now in Jesus' name.

In the name of Jesus, I take authority over these emotional triggers over the emotional stimuli over all *gears* and *mechanisms* that connect them to each other, over all mental images, over every trigger and every demon behind these triggers now in Jesus' name. Now take a deep breath and say out loud, Go! In Jesus' name.

> **Lord, thank you for freeing my mind from these triggers and associated demons. I ask you to come in, take and fill the place where they existed and the next time the enemy tries to trigger something in my mind, I will remember how you set me free today and stand in my sound mind, sound emotions, and declare my freedom openly in Jesus' name. Amen.**

Chapter 7
Demonic Nature in the Deeds of the Flesh

So God created man in His own image; in the image of God He created him; male and female He created them. **Genesis 1:27 (NKJV)**

But Satan wanted them in his image so he tempted Adam and Eve to fall to sin.

Then the serpent said to the woman, "You will not surely die. For God knows that in the day you eat of it your eyes will be opened, and you will be like God, knowing good and evil." So when the woman saw that the tree was good for food, that it was pleasant to the eyes, and a tree desirable to make one wise, she took of its fruit and ate. She also gave to her husband with her, and he ate. Then the eyes of both of them were opened, and they knew that they were naked; and they sewed fig leaves together and made themselves coverings. And they heard the sound of the LORD God walking in the garden in the cool of the day, and Adam and his wife hid themselves from the presence of the LORD God among the trees of the garden. **Genesis 3:4-8**

To the woman God said: "I will greatly multiply your sorrow and your conception; In pain you shall bring forth children; Your desire shall be for your husband, And he shall rule over you." Then to Adam He said, "Because you have heeded the voice of your wife, and have eaten from the tree of which I commanded you, saying, 'You shall not eat of it': " Cursed is the ground for your sake; In toil you shall eat of it All the days of your life. Both thorns and thistles it shall bring forth for you, And you shall eat the herb of the field In the sweat of your face you shall eat bread Till you return to the ground, For out of it you were taken; For dust you are, And to dust you shall return." Genesis 3:16-19 (NKJV)

The New Testament gives us a clearer understanding of the consequences of the fall.

Therefore, just as through one man sin entered the world, and death through sin, and thus death spread to all men, because all sinned. Romans 5:12 (NKJV)

...so that as sin reigned in death, even so grace might reign through righteousness to eternal life through Jesus Christ our Lord. Romans 5:21 (NKJV)

In the Old Testament, the word flesh (basar) is often interpreted to mean the physical body or mankind or animal kind. In the New Testament, depending on the context of the scripture, flesh (sarx) could mean physical body (as opposed to the spirit or soul) or also mean the fleshly appetites of humans that have not been surrendered to God.

Satan's nature entered the world through Adam's sin and every one from that time forward received a cursed nature, a flesh nature, the nature of Satan, self love, self centeredness, selfishness, the "I will" *pride-full* nature of Satan. Grace, however, re-entered the world through Jesus Christ.

So today, even though we were created in the image of God, the whole world walks in likeness to the image of Satan's cursed nature until they see and receive the gospel of Jesus and **repent, turn from their sins.**

The word *"flesh"* in Romans 8:7 means the carnal attitudes, thoughts, desires that are not surrendered to God:

*...because the mind set on the **flesh** is **hostile (enmity)** toward God; for it does not subject itself to the law of*

God, for it is not even able to do so, Romans 8:7 (NASB)

Here is the meaning for **hostile** found in Strong's Concordance #2189 in the Greek; <u>echthra</u> *ekh'-thrah* feminine of 2190; hostility; by implication, a reason for opposition:--**enmity,** hatred.

The unsurrendered fleshly mind set on the fleshly desires will not submit to God's law. It is basically at war with God. Man's fleshly mindset has aligned itself with the devil. Just like the devil, man's fleshly mindset is hostile to God and won't submit itself to the laws of God. The devil, though, is resolute in his hostility, but man can still repent.

Galatians 5:16-21 addresses the deeds and works of the flesh:

> *I say then: Walk in the Spirit, and you shall not fulfill the lust of the flesh. For the flesh lusts against the Spirit, and the Spirit against the flesh; and these are contrary to one another, so that you do not do the things that you wish. But if you are led by the Spirit, you are not under the law.*
>
> *Now the works of the flesh are evident, which are: adultery, fornication, uncleanness, lewdness, idolatry, sorcery, hatred, contentions, jealousies, outbursts of wrath, selfish ambitions, dissensions, heresies, envy, murders, drunkenness, revelries, and the like; of which I tell you beforehand, just as I also told you in time past, that those who practice such things will not inherit the kingdom of God.*

These deeds represent the character and nature of the devil. That is why we are told to put to death the deeds of the flesh in Romans 8:13:

> *For if you live according to the flesh you will die; but if by the Spirit you put to death the deeds of the body, you*

will live. (NKJV)

We put to death the deeds of the flesh **not** to make us feel better, but because we want to put to death the nature and character of the devil that manifest in our bodies, so we can live.

Jeremiah 17:9 describes the condition of man after the fall. *"The **heart** is deceitful above all things, And desperately **wicked**; who can know it?* (NKJV) Because the heart is wicked, the deeds are wicked. Whatever proceeds from a person either from their mouth or from their deeds, comes from their heart. Jeremiah spoke of a New Covenant that God would make with his people: *"...I will put my law within them and on their **heart** I will write it; and I will be their God, and they shall be my people.* Jer. 31:33 (NKJV) This prophetically speaks of a relationship with God after the cross.

Whatever is in a person will eventually flow out from that person. Jesus said in Mark 7:21-23:

For from within, out of the heart of men, proceed evil thoughts, adulteries, fornications, murders, thefts, covetousness, wickedness, deceit, lewdness, an evil eye, blasphemy, pride, foolishness. All these evil things come from within and defile a man." (NKJV)

Jesus said you can judge a tree by the fruit it bears. *Even so, every good **tree** bears good **fruit**, but a bad **tree** bears bad **fruit**....for a **tree** is known by its **fruit**.* Matthew 7:17, 12:33 (NKJV) He also said in Luke 6:45

A good man out of the good treasure of his heart brings forth good; and an evil man out of the evil treasure of his heart brings forth evil. For out of the abundance of the heart his mouth speaks. (NKJV)

You will recognize the selfish or (even demonic nature) of a person by the fruit he bears and what comes forth from his mouth. This self-life is born of the flesh and those who live by it and let it rule them, will use and try to control everyone around them because they seek their own selfish interest.

If a person loves to satisfy his flesh more than he loves God, then that self centeredness will fill his heart, and it will be evident to all. The Bible says *Therefore submit to God. Resist the devil and he will flee from you.* James 4:7(NKJV)

God rules (masters) you in repentance as you turn from sin; from the flesh. Satan rules and masters you when your flesh rules. If you want God to rule you and be master over you, then you have to live in a surrendered mode. That is, a mode of being always willing and ready to surrender to God and then turn away from sin and escape from it.

Here is some really great news from the Word of God.

No temptation has overtaken you except such as is common to man; but God is faithful, who will not allow you to be tempted beyond what you are able, but with the temptation will also make the way of escape, that you may be able to bear it. 1 Corinthians 10:13 (NKJV)

A person who has been crucified with Christ, buried with Him in the waters of baptism, and has risen with Him in newness of life, has a new nature and becomes a totally different person as he yields to the Holy Spirit instead rather than his fleshly impulses. By practicing repentance daily he is learning how to turn away from sin.

"I have been crucified with Christ; and it is no longer I who live, but Christ lives in me; and the life which I now live in the flesh I live by faith in the Son of God, who loved me and gave Himself up for me. Gal. 2:20 (NKJV)

...having been buried with Him in baptism, in which you were also raised up with Him through faith in the working of God, who raised Him from the dead. Col.

2:12 (NKJV)

If then you were raised with Christ, seek those things which are above, where Christ is sitting at the right hand of God. Set your mind on things above, not on things on the earth for you died, and your life has been hidden with Christ in God. Col. 3:1-3 (NKJV)

When we consistently surrender ourselves to Him, then the Spirit of God is able to lead instead of the flesh leading. The indwelling Holy Spirit empowers us to put to death the deeds of the flesh, nailing that fleshly desire to the cross. Then, as it says in Ephesians 6:10, & 13-18:

Vs. 10 Finally, my brothers, be strong in the Lord and in the power of His might.

*Therefore, take up the full armor of God, so that you will be able to resist in the **evil day** and **having done everything, to stand firm. Stand firm therefore,** HAVING GIRDED YOUR LOINS WITH TRUTH, and HAVING PUT ON THE BREASTPLATE OF RIGHTEOUSNESS,*

and having shod your feet with the PREPARATION OF THE GOSPEL OF PEACE;

in addition to all, taking up the SHIELD OF FAITH with which you will be able to extinguish all the flaming arrows of the evil one.

And take THE HELMET OF SALVATION, and the SWORD OF
THE SPIRIT, which is the WORD OF GOD,

With all prayer and petition pray at all times in the Spirit, and with this in view, be on the alert with all perseverance and petition for all the saints,

Family, pay particular attention to verses 13 and 14,....*having done everything, to stand, stand firm therefore.* (NKJV)

James 4:7 summarizes this exhortation: *Therefore submit to God.* ***Resist*** *the* ***devil*** *and he will flee from you.*

Many of us have lazily done little or none of this and that is why we habitually find ourselves walking in the deeds of the flesh. Oh, we may have resisted the devil, but we haven't first submitted to God and we have not prepared ourselves with the gospel of peace; (reading God's word for ourselves, listening for God to speak to us). Also, we have not learned to use our faith when the enemy sticks us with his arrows, for when troubles, trials and temptation come, we do not immediately run back to the day of our salvation in Jesus Christ and remember that we are saved from it all, nor are we in constant prayer for ourselves and others.

So you can see, it is easy to stay in the flesh when you haven't done all to stand firm against the enemy in the evil day.

Let's look at the nature of the devil. Jesus said in John 10:10 that he comes to steal, kill and destroy. One of the ways he accomplishes this is through the prideful attitudes that man reflects from the fall. Look at what is said about the devil in Isaiah 14:12- 14 (NKJV):

> *"How you are fallen from heaven, O Lucifer, son of the morning!*
> *How you are cut down to the ground, You who weakened the nations!*
> *For you have said in your heart: "****I will*** *ascend into heaven,*
> ***I will*** *exalt my throne above the stars of God;* ***I will*** *also sit on the mount of the congregation On*

> *the farthest sides of the north;*
> ***I will*** *ascend above the heights of the clouds,*
> ***I will*** *be like the Most High."*

These five "**I wills**" show the prideful arrogance of Satan. This is also what is reflected in the fall of man. If anyone comes to God through Jesus Christ and has not repented and turned from pride, he is still walking in rebellion. He is still deciding for himself what is good and what is evil, based on his personal desires. That person is really saying in his heart, "I will not give up pride, because I love pride and self more than I love God."

Contrast that with the nature of God expressed in Exodus34:5-7

> *Now the LORD descended in the cloud and stood with him (Moses) there, and proclaimed the name of the LORD. And the LORD passed before him and proclaimed,*
> ***"The LORD, the LORD God, merciful and gracious, longsuffering, and abounding in goodness and truth, keeping mercy for thousands, forgiving iniquity and transgression and sin,*** *by no means clearing the guilty, visiting the iniquity of the fathers upon the children and the children's children to the third and the fourth generation."* (NKJV)

See how God's nature is good and the nature of Satan is evil. When someone in the crowd asked Jesus what was the greatest commandment, he answered:

> *Jesus said to him, '"You shall love the LORD your God with all your heart, with all your soul, and with all your mind.' This is the first and great commandment. And the*

second *is* like it: *'You shall love your neighbor as yourself.'* Matt. 22:37-39 (NKJV)

A person can't obey that commandment if he loves his prideful, greedy, selfish flesh. Pride is at the root of many sins. Pride wants to be the center of attention. Pride receives glory from men. Pride is always concerned with its own image. Pride always has to be right. Pride loves the approval of men more than the approval of God. Pride welcomes the thoughts from Satan to build one's own self image.

Greed is much like pride and is in the same family tree. Greed loves the things of the world. Greed hoards to build its fleshly kingdom. Greed, like pride, is a lust of the flesh. The Bible says this about these lusts which are of the world and not of God:

> *Do not love the world or the things in the world. If anyone loves the world, the love of the Father is not in him. For all that is in the world—the lust of the flesh, the lust of the eyes, and the pride of life—is not of the Father but is of the world. and the world is passing away, and the lust of it; but he who does the will of God abides forever.* 1John 2:15-17 (NKJV)

When I became a Christian, I purposed in my heart that I would have no other influence in my life outside of the Holy Spirit, whom Jesus sent. I quickly had to decide who is master; me or Jesus. Anyone can have 100 fleshly ideas mulling around in our heads and we can decide to act on them, but not one of them came from our master Jesus, because they are flesh.

I remember when I was a young boy one summer vacation in Connecticut, thinking it would be fun to run down a big hill. It was steep and as I ran quickly I gained speed. Soon, I was going faster than my feet could run. As I came to a small dip, I dropped 15 feet and tumbled the rest of the way down. I broke my collar bone and things quickly changed for the summer vacation. I was sent home to Florida to heal.

What had seemed like a good idea, took on a life of its own and soon I was caught in its momentum. I have found this principle to be a constant truth in my life. Just like a pebble that is thrown into a pond that causes a ripple effect, to have an effect on the whole pond, so is any action of the flesh. Galatians 6:8 says: *For he who sows to his **flesh** will of the **flesh reap** corruption, but he who sows to the Spirit will of the Spirit **reap** everlasting life.* (NKJV)

Jesus gives us a way to test the flesh in Luke 6:27-36 (NKJV):

"But I say to you who hear: Love your enemies, do good to those who hate you, bless those who curse you, and pray for those who spitefully use you. To him who strikes you on the one cheek, offer the other also. And from him who takes away your cloak, do not withhold your tunic either. Give to everyone who asks of you. And from him who takes away your goods do not ask them back. And just as you want men to do to you, you also do to them likewise.

"But if you love those who love you, what credit is that to you? For even sinners love those who love them. And if you do good to those who do good to you, what credit is that to you? For even sinners do the same. And if you lend to those from whom you hope to receive back, what credit is that to you? For even sinners lend to sinners to receive as much back.

But love your enemies, do good, and lend, hoping for nothing in return; and your reward will be great, and you will be sons of the Most High. For He is kind to the unthankful and evil. Therefore be merciful, just as your Father also is merciful.

This message is for ALL the disciples of Jesus Christ for all the ages to come. The reason this sounds foreign to us is because it doesn't fit into the fleshly standard of Christianity that we have cultivated for our lives. Over the course of our lives, we have created fleshly demonic inspired attitudes.

Earlier I quoted Matthew 22:37-39 (NKJV)

Jesus said to him, "'You shall love the LORD your God with all your heart, with all your soul, and with all your mind.' This is the first and great commandment. And the second is like it: 'You shall love your neighbor as yourself.'"

O, I love God with all my heart, and He knows that I love him, but how can I love my neighbor who turned into an enemy, who cursed me, who used me, who stole from me? This is where the rubber meets the road. This is the flesh test. The way these types of things are handled, show us and the world what nature is living inside of us. Be it the rejecting judgment of Satan or the unconditional love of God.

The powers of darkness tempt every Christian to walk after the lust of his own flesh and to hate his neighbor who offends them. The powers of darkness that we wrestle with are found in Eph. 6:12 *…against principalities, against powers, against the rulers of the darkness of this age, against spiritual hosts of wickedness in the heavenly places,* **oppress, harass, and influence** us from the outside and from the inside.

Because we automatically have from our flesh thoughts that tempt our minds with anger, hate, resentment, jealousy, criticism, fault finding un-forgiveness, etc. we need to consider the following words of Paul in 2 Corinthians 10:3-6 (NKJV):

For though we walk in the flesh, we do not war

according to the flesh. For the weapons of our warfare are not carnal but mighty in God for pulling down strongholds, casting down arguments and every high thing that exalts itself against the knowledge of God, bringing every thought into captivity to the obedience of Christ, and being ready to punish all disobedience when your obedience is fulfilled.

Many times, I have had to stop in the middle of doing something and pull an ungodly, fleshly, demonic thought down out of my mind and command it to leave my thinking in the name of Jesus. It is essential that we stop these fleshly thoughts while they are still in our minds, so they won't work their way into sin.

But each one is tempted when he is drawn away by his own desires and enticed. Then, when desire has conceived, it gives birth to sin; and sin, when it is full-grown, brings forth death. Do not be deceived, my beloved brethren. James 1:14-16 (NKJV)

Why does it say *Do not be deceived, my beloved brethren?* Because many have done this, that is, from a thought, they have fallen into the flesh and into sin. These thought are the very opposite to good, to God, to love. They are the schemes of the enemy to keep us in the fleshly, demonic deeds of the flesh.

We must remember to stand against the appetites of the flesh. That begins in our minds, as in Colossians 3:2-10 (NKJV)

Set your mind on things above, not on things on the earth. For you died, and your life is hidden with Christ in God. When Christ who is our life appears, then you also will appear with Him in glory.

Therefore put to death your members which are on the earth: fornication, uncleanness, passion, evil desire, and covetousness, which is idolatry. Because of these things the wrath of God is coming upon the sons of disobedience, in which you yourselves once walked when you lived in them.

But now you yourselves are to put off all these: anger, wrath, malice, blasphemy, filthy language out of your mouth. Do not lie to one another, since you have put off the old man with his deeds, and have put on the new man who is renewed in knowledge according to the image of Him who created him,

God gives us a serious warning about flesh-led living in Romans8:13-14 (NKJV):

For if you live according to the flesh you will die; but if by the Spirit you put to death the deeds of the body, you will live. For as many as are led by the Spirit of God, these are sons of God.

I have never preached *Cotton Candy Christianity.* You can not have fleshly Christianity. The purpose of the cross was not that we should continue to live in sin, but that we should die to self and therefore die to sin.

*Then Jesus said to His disciples, "If anyone desires to come after Me, let him deny himself, and take up his **cross**, and **follow** Me.* Matt. 16:24 (NKJV)

All four gospels admonish us that we should deny ourselves if we are to follow Him. Denying means to die to fleshly desires and be ready to be nailed to the cross with Jesus. Making Jesus Christ your LIFE, means giving up everything of the flesh. Everything? Yes everything. How much do you love Jesus? Enough to die to our flesh for Him? Dying to the fleshly nature can be quick and easy, by just a firm decision to quit living by the flesh. Some call it "Going cold turkey," "going all the way or nothing at all."

Therefore, since Christ suffered for us in the flesh, arm

> *yourselves also with the same mind, for he who has suffered in the flesh has ceased from sin,* 1 Peter 4:1 (NKJV)

In other words, sin loses its power when you decide to deny the flesh so it won't master you.

> *For when we were in the flesh, the sinful passions which were aroused by the law were at work in our members to bear fruit to death.* Romans 7:5 (NKJV)

Being alive to the flesh puts you back under the Law which causes you to CRAVE the appetites of the flesh, which brings you back to death.

> *There is therefore now no condemnation to those who are in Christ Jesus, **who do not walk according to the flesh,** but according to the Spirit. For the law of the Spirit of life in Christ Jesus has made me free from the law of sin and death.* Romans 8:1-2 (NKJV)

Note that there is <u>no condemnation</u> to those who <u>do not</u> walk according to the flesh. This implies that <u>there is condemnation</u> to those who <u>do</u> walk according to the flesh. The neat part is that the minute you make a decision to obey the law of the Spirit of life in Christ by denying the flesh, Jesus sets you free from the law of sin and death.

The law of the Spirit of Life in Christ Jesus is simply this, if you are a Christian, you have been crucified with Christ. You are not supposed to be making your own decisions any more. You are supposed to pass them all through Christ.

> *I have been crucified with Christ and I no longer live, but Christ lives in me. The life I now live in the body, I live by faith in the Son of God, who loved me and gave himself for me.* Galatians 2:20 (NIV)

> *Therefore if you have been raised up with Christ, keep*

seeking the things above, where Christ is seated at the right hand of God. Set your mind on the things above, not on the things that are on earth, for you have died and your life is hidden with Christ in God. When Christ, who is our life, is revealed, then you also will be revealed with Him in glory. Therefore consider the members of your earthly body as dead to immorality, impurity, passion, evil desire, and greed, which amount to idolatry. Colossians 3:1-5 (NASB)

As we continue to surrender to Christ, moment by moment, we change our desires and our appetites and put to death our former appetites for sin. Satan's enticements no longer rule in us because we now have a new nature empowered by God's indwelling spirit who reigns in our mortal bodies.

This transformation doesn't happen automatically but as we lay aside our self-centered desires as Paul writes to the Ephesians in chapter 4:22-24...*that, in reference to your former manner of life, you lay aside the old self, which is being corrupted in accordance with the **lusts of deceit**, and that you be renewed in the spirit of your mind, and put on the new self, which in the likeness of God has been created **in righteousness and holiness of the truth.*** (NASB)

In this passage we can see that there are two courses of action for a believer. He can continue to follow the behavior of his former self
– with a flesh-led nature or he can live according to his new self – with a Holy Spirit led nature.

Look at some of those key words: Old self - **Lust of deceit**; New self – **in the likeness of God... in righteousness and holiness of the truth**. Let's look closer – the old man is filled or corrupted with the **lust of deceit.** Deceit means misrepresentation; falsehood; intentional fraud; betrayal; double dealing; trickery; insecurity; mislead; cheat. The old nature – fed by the appetites of the flesh- lusted after these things.

The new man, born again with his Holy Spirit led nature, puts off the deeds of the flesh and operates in **righteousness** and in **holiness of the truth.**

Righteousness means; just, pious, guiltless, pure, ruled by what is right.

Holiness means; set apart, sacred, consecrated, dedicated, free of sin, untainted by sin, devoted to God, innocent.

Truth means- the true or actual state of a matter, the state or character of being true, the principal of right.

As born-again Christians with a new nature, we still must choose between the appetites of our flesh and the leading of the Holy Spirit who now indwells us – a process that becomes easier as we daily surrender ourselves to the Lord and are conformed into his likeness.

There are several things I want to remind you of. First, deliverance from demons is a process by which we kick out the enemy, preventing him from manifesting his nature in our flesh, thus making it easier to be it renewed in the spirit of our minds. Second, baptism is a process of acknowledging that our old nature is dead and buried with Christ. It is a point of reference when your flesh tries to rule.

Therefore we have been buried with Him through baptism into death, so that as Christ was raised from the dead through the glory of the Father, so we too might walk in newness of life.

*For if we have become **united with Him in the likeness of His death**,*
certainly we shall also be in the likeness of His resurrection,

> *knowing this, that our old self was crucified with Him, in order that our body of sin might be done away with, so that we would no longer be slaves to sin; Romans 6:4-6 (NASB)*

Family, the devil does not want us to walk in newness of life as Spirit-led renewed believers. He wants us to walk in the flesh, because he can entice us through our soulish desires.

> *I say then: Walk in the Spirit, and you shall not fulfill the lust of the flesh. For the flesh lusts against the Spirit, and the Spirit against the flesh; and these are contrary to one another, so that you do not do the things that you wish.* ***But if you are led by the Spirit, you are not under the law.***

> *Now the works of the flesh are evident, which are: adultery, fornication, uncleanness, lewdness, idolatry, sorcery, hatred, contentions, jealousies, outbursts of wrath, selfish ambitions, dissensions, heresies, envy, murders, drunkenness, revelries, and the like; of which I tell you beforehand, just as I also told you in time past, that those who practice such things will not inherit the kingdom of God.*

> *But the fruit of the Spirit is love, joy, peace, longsuffering, kindness, goodness, faithfulness, gentleness, self-control. Against such there is no law.*
> Galatians 5:16-23 (NKJV)

Just a little note to those who wink at practicing sin because they are under the blood of Jesus: This letter by Paul was written to believers in Christ. Verse 18 is true and what it implies the (opposite) is also true. When Paul says that if we are led by the Spirit, we are not under the law, he implies that if we are not led by the Spirit, that is, when we are led by the flesh, we place ourselves back under the law.

There is constant warfare between the Spirit led man and the fleshly led soul of man. Satan and his demons launch their battle from the flesh and spearhead warfare against the Holy Spirit reborn areas of a man. Paul describes this in scriptures as a constant raging battle.

Demons for the most part, arouse and inflame areas of the flesh of a believer to make him or her fall back into carnal ways, to practice them, so that they can entice believers away from being Holy Spirit led. But as Galatians 5:18 says, if you are led by the Spirit, you are not under the law.

In Luke's gospel, Jesus revealed the judgmental attitudes operating in His disciples. We often fall into the same holier-than- thou attitudes today.

> *Now it came to pass, when the time had come for Him to be received up, that He steadfastly set His face to go to Jerusalem, and sent messengers before His face. And as they went, they entered a village of the Samaritans, to prepare for Him. But they did not receive Him, because His face was set for the journey to Jerusalem. And when His disciples James and John saw this, they said, "Lord, do You want us to command fire to come down from heaven and consume them, just as Elijah did?"*
>
> *But He turned and rebuked them, and said, "You do not know what manner of spirit you are of. For the Son of Man did not come to destroy men's lives but to save them." And they went to another village.* Luke 9:51-56 (NKJV)

Jesus rebuked James and John saying, "You do not know what kind of spirit you are of." He was insinuating that they were operating out of a spirit other than the Holy Spirit.

What was operating in them and through them was not the Lord. The words they spoke evidenced an attitude that was contrary to the Spirit of Christ. They were manifesting something that originated as a temptation by an evil spirit, it enticed their flesh to consider themselves superior to the Samaritans, and as a result, they were serving the demon spirits.

They manifested a racist spirit of intolerance, bigotry, prejudice, spite, and hatred towards the Samaritans, and apparently it didn't matter if hundreds of innocent people died as long as they could take revenge for the offense they received when they and their master Jesus were rejected.

Did any of you ever take an offense and something rose up in you and you said out loud or just in your heart, "Nuke–em Lord." You sort out the righteous one later. You see, Family, that attitude came from the flesh operating deep within the soul where unclean spirits are at work to manipulate our thinking so they can manifest and work through us. Sometimes they even speak to our minds in the first person ("I hate him!") so that we think those are our thoughts. But they are temptations to accept those thoughts as our own.

Jesus had to remind those two disciples that he did not come to destroy men's lives, but to save men's lives. Those two men were supposed to be manifesting THAT. What was THAT? *Healing, Deliverance, and Salvation* coming to town. That was the attitude that they were supposed to have but something else was surfacing from them.

Many times, something else surfaces from us too, that is of a demonic spirit. When we have been abused, belittled, rejected, then our first fleshly impulse is to get angry, get even, seek revenge, "I'll show them, I'll do this or that and it will hurt them back." That is when we are motivated by a different spirit that came from the flesh that is in opposition to the Spirit of God.

These are several scriptures where believers were influenced by demons and acted it out in the flesh.

When Jesus predicts His death and resurrection and speaks to Peter:

> *"Get behind Me, Satan! You are an offense to Me, for you are not mindful of the things of God, but the things of men."* Matt 16:21-23 (NKJV)

In other words, you have your mind on fleshly things.

Peter discerned that Satan had filled Ananias' and Sapphira's hearts to lie to the Holy Spirit about the sale price of their property.

> *But Peter said, "Ananias, why has Satan filled your heart to lie to the Holy Spirit and keep back part of the price of the land for yourself?* In Acts 5:3 (NKJV)

They were filled with covetousness when keeping back part of the price of the land. As a result of their deception, they both fell over dead. (Acts 5:3-10)

When Peter spoke to Simon the magician who was a new convert and believed in Jesus in and wanted to buy the power of the Holy Spirit, Peter said to him:

> *Thou hast neither part nor lot in this matter: for thy heart is not right in the sight of God. Repent therefore of this thy wickedness, and pray God, if perhaps the thought of thine heart may be forgiven thee. For I perceive that thou art in the gall of bitterness, and in the bond of iniquity.* Acts 8:21-23 Acts 8:9-24 (KJV)

Peter saw that this new believer had a bitter heart. He warned Simon that he was **poisoned by bitterness and wrapped up, tied up by iniquity."** Peter spoke from his own personal experience, when, in Luke's account, we can see that Satan had access to Peter's mind and mouth. In similar ways, we all have been used by the enemy who operates from our flesh.

> *And the Lord said, Simon, Simon, behold, Satan has desired you, that he may sift you as wheat. But I have prayed for you, that your faith fail not. And when you are converted, strengthen your brothers. And he said to Him, Lord, I am ready to go with You, both into prison and into death.*
>
> *And He said, I say to you, Peter, the cock shall not crow this day before you shall deny knowing Me three times.* Luke 22:31-34 (MKJV)

Another example is when Jesus spoke about Judas Iscariot who was filled with greed:

> *Jesus answered them, "Did I not choose you, the twelve, and one of you is a devil?"* John 6:70 (NKJV)

In 2 Tim. 1:7 Paul wrote to a young believer, Timothy, encouraging him to stand against a spirit of fear. Fear is an emotion. It started as a spiritual attack that stirred up fear in his flesh. Paul wrote other believers about this as well.

In his letter to the Roman church, Paul also writes about the enticements of the flesh that lead to bondage and death:

> *Therefore, brethren, we are debtors—not to the flesh, to live according to the flesh. For if you live according to the flesh you will die; but if by the Spirit you put to death the deeds of the body, you will live. For as many as are led by the Spirit of God, these are sons of God. For you did not receive the spirit of bondage again to fear, but you received the Spirit of adoption by whom we cry out, "Abba, Father."* Romans 8:12-15 (NKJV)

There are spirits at work fueled by our flesh that try to

pull believers back into chains of bondage. The spirit of slavery is a spirit of bondage, and it can not only lead to fear, but it can lead to addiction, lust, anger, gossip, or bondage to any sin. Satan will try to bring all believers back into chains of bondage, back into fleshly living. The devil will use anything from our flesh to bring us back into bondage and death.

Before we go into deliverance let me remind promises to all believers:

> *And these signs will follow those who believe: In My name they will cast out demons; they will speak with new tongues; they will take up serpents; and if they drink anything deadly, it will by no means hurt them; they will lay hands on the sick, and they will recover*

> *Assuredly, I say to you, whatever you bind on earth will be bound in heaven, and whatever you loose on earth will be loosed in heaven. Again I say to you that if two of you agree on earth concerning anything that they ask, it will be done for them by My Father in heaven.* Matt 18:17-19 (NKJV)

> *Behold, I give you the authority to trample on serpents and scorpions, and over all the power of the enemy, and nothing shall by any means hurt you.* Luke 10:19 (NKJV)

Next, we are going to cast out all unclean, evil, demonic spirits that have afflicted you, harassed you, and influenced you. They come out in the name of Jesus and they come out on the breath. When Jesus cast them out, they came out in a loud voice. There is a lot of breath that is expelled in order to make a loud voice. It is interesting to note that in the "Vines Complete Expository Dictionary," the Greek word for spirit and breath is the same word. ("pneuma"). When Jesus was casting out spirits, a lot of "pneuma" was expelled, that is breath/spirit. So in this deliverance, as a act of your will, I will ask you to blow out breath in the name of Jesus to start the process of (evil) "spirits" leaving.

Speak the following aloud:

In the name of Jesus Christ, I command out of me all spirits that are hostile towards God:

Adultery, fornication, uncleanness, lewdness, idolatry, sorcery, hatred, contentions, outbursts of wrath, selfish ambitions, dissensions, heresies, envy, murders, drunkenness, revelries. Go in Jesus' name. (Blow out breath). Leave in Jesus' name.

In the name of Jesus, I command out of me:

Evil thoughts, adulteries, fornications, thefts, covetousness, greed, wickedness, deceit, lewdness, spirit of the evil eye, blasphemy, pride, foolishness, spirit of slavery to bondage, bitterness, spirits that are attached to iniquity, transgression and sins, spirit of offense, rejection, anger and pride by being insulted, a racist spirit of intolerance, bigotry, prejudice, spite, and hatred towards another nationality, lust of deceit, condemnation self- condemnation, guilt, shame, misrepresentation; falsehood; intentional fraud; betrayal; double dealing; trickery; insecurity; mislead; cheat; spirit that makes me CRAVE.. (name your CRAVING ……..), uncleanness, passion for evil desire, and covetousness, idolatry, disobedience, unthankful, ungrateful, selfishness, pride of life. Go in Jesus' name. (Blow out breath). Leave in Jesus' name.

In the name of Jesus, I command out of me:

Rejection, envy, jealousy, suspicion, paranoia, anger, deception, murder, fear control, witchcraft, accusation, perverseness, self pity, pouting, bitterness, resentment, false compassion, compulsive behavior, self accusations, deception, lying, possessiveness, rebellion, divination, division, divorce, depression, discouragement, despair, hopelessness, suicide, vanity scorner, scoffer, sexually dysfunctional, torment, terror, fantasy, self hate, perfection, acute anxiety, panic disorder, chronic anxiety, hyperventilation syndrome, bondage, egotism, intolerance, frustration, death. Go in Jesus' name. (Blow out breath). Leave in Jesus' name.

In the name of Jesus, I command out of me:

Violence, unteachable, gluttony, alcoholism, shame, religious spirits, fear of man, selfishness, distrust, sociopath, psychopath, lust of the world, dysfunctional, addicted to sports, addicted to movies, addicted to books, addicted to the internet, no sex drive, rape, unclean thoughts, vain imaginations, escape, lust for power, for position, for money, arrested development in spiritual growth, in mental growth, in emotional growth, in physical growth, seduction, lust, control, bulimia, anorexia, witchcraft, nymphomania, gigolo, whoremonger, sexual abuse, child abuse, rape, child molestation, sarcasm, narcissus, hate, fornication, poverty, dyslexia. Go in Jesus' name. (Blow out breath). Leave in Jesus' name.

In the name of Jesus, I command out of me:

Bestiality, incest, stubbornness, disrespect, machismo, greed, self worship, lust for material things, addiction to shopping, drugs, food, gossip, miser, penny pincher, hoarder, accumulation, pack rat, homosexuality, mind control, condemnation, bondage to abusive relationships, cannot accept responsibility, failure, vagabond, insecurity, phobias to germs, crowds, fear of the dark, memory problems, fatigue, bitterness, slumber, tiredness, sleeping all the time, nit picking, perfection, vanity, critical spirit, Obsessive Compulsive Behavior, checking, re-checking, obsessive planner, obsessive cleaner, obsessive counting, re-counting, self hatred, false responsibility, resisting, foot dragging, punishment using time schedules, punishment using sex, punishment using rejection, intolerance, conceit, projection of blame anti-Christ, legalism, spirits that cause confusion, inability to concentrate, decreased attention span, memory loss, cloudy thinking, drowsiness, headaches. Go in Jesus' name. (Blow out breath). Leave in Jesus' name.

In the name of Jesus, I command out of me:

Rejection, abandonment, failure, negativity, pessimism, judgmental, opposition, condemnation, guilt, criticism, betrayal, fear of commitment, fear of responsibility, fear of authority, fear of diseases, fear of darkness, fear of being alone, fear of death, fear of being closed in, fear of a sound, fear of foods, fear of certain words (Name your own fears....) Go in Jesus' name (Blow out breath). Leave in Jesus' name.

In the name of Jesus, I command out of me:

Selfishness, superiority, controlling, vanity, overbearing, boastful, rebellious, conceited, selfish ambition, rudeness, man-pleaser, insolent, always right, insensitive, presumptuous, arrogant, self love, self righteous, spirit that wants attention, haughty, self interest, unloving, self glory, egotistical, I, I, I, ME, ME, ME spirit, possessiveness. Go in Jesus' name. (Blow out breath). Leave in Jesus' name.

In the name of Jesus, I command out of me:

Punishment, discontentment, dishonor to self, to others, fear of loosing honor, fear of being punished, hopelessness, helplessness, humiliation, put down, ridicule, failure, stupid thinking, stupid decisions, senseless mind, foolishness, lack of knowledge, lack of wisdom. Go in Jesus' name. (Blow out breath0. Leave in Jesus' name.

In the name of Jesus, I command out of me:
Sexual idolatry, homosexuality, greed, troubled heart, poverty of spirit, poverty of soul, poverty of the body, lack, insufficiency, pride, trouble receiving, trouble maker, attention seeking, callousness, hard hearted, cruelty, revenge, cold love, cold shoulder, punishing others, ungratefulness, false front denial, stealing, lying, dishonesty, stretching the truth, craftiness, schemer, always controlling and maneuvering others. Go in Jesus' name (Blow out breath). Leave in Jesus' name.

In Jesus' name, I command out of me:
Rudeness, traitor, cowardice, turmoil, muddled mind, forgetfulness, superiority, depression, flashbacks, painful thoughts, escape, hysteria, losing control, withdrawal, nervousness, loss of concentration, sloppiness, temper, irritation, hostility, bitter love, self centeredness. Go in Jesus' name. (Blow out breath). Leave in Jesus' name.

In Jesus' name, I command out of me:
Addiction, addictiveness, bad habits, ungodly compulsions and cravings, slavery or bondage to sin, procrastination, nervousness stress, tension, distrust, unreliability, fear of looking stupid, self hate for wrong decisions, abuse, self abuse, emotional abuse, mental abuse, physical abuse, sexual abuse, anger. Go in Jesus' name. (Blow out breath). Leave in Jesus' name.

In the name of Jesus, I command out of me:
Guilt, rage, out of control anger, pain, sickness, compromise, intellectualism, egotism, bragging, pride, automatic response, accident prone, self destruction, all spirits of pride, defiance, haughtiness, self-righteousness, criticism, judgmental, murmuring, grumbling, complaining, rebellion, contention, fighting, competition, vanity, self worship, arrogance, insolent, discontent, doctorial,

egotistical, bragging, mockery, self accession, self-promotion, exaggeration, flattery, lover of power, perfectionism, stubbornness, anger, rage, temper, violence, murder, and the source of all these demons to leave me now in Jesus' name. Take a deep breath and cough them out. Go in Jesus' name.

In the name of Jesus Christ, I command out of me every:

Anti-Christ spirit, anti-God spirit, every spirit that rejects God, the bride of Satan, the prince of darkness. Take a deep breath and cough them out. Go in Jesus' name.

In the name of Jesus Christ, I command out of me:

All spirits of rejection, fear of being rejected, self rejection, spirits that make me feel unloved, unwanted, not needed, insecurity, inferiority, and all like spirits. Take a deep breath and cough them out. Go in Jesus' name.

In the name of Jesus Christ, I command out of me:

Spirits of loneliness, depression, lost hope, despair, self pity, despondency, desperation, discouragement, hopelessness, isolation, spirits that make me feel like pulling back, pulling out, giving up, defeated, sunkenness, dullness, flattened, let down, criminal minded, wrong thinking, insanity, madness, suicide, spirit of death. Take a deep breath and cough them out. Go in Jesus' name.

In the name of Jesus Christ, I command out of me:

All spirits of lying, spirits of error, lust of the eyes, pride of life, self love, narcissism, self-righteousness, spirits that puff up, show off, braggart, boastful, egotistical, haughty, high-minded, vanity, show-off, cursing, blasphemy, and all like spirits. Take a deep breath and cough them out. Go in Jesus' name.

In the name of Jesus Christ, I command out of me:

Evil spirits of delusion, fixed false beliefs, delirium, delusional disorder, illusion, paranoia, hallucinations, schizophrenia, bipolar disorder, distress, disturbed mind, betrayed reasoning, covetousness, foolishness, folly, ambition greed, self worship, idolatry, self deception, self delusion, selfish desires, fixed misconceptions. Take a deep breath and cough them out. Go in Jesus' name.

In the name of Jesus, I command out of me all spirits of:

Religious error, every spirit of defeatism, witchcraft, unbelief, doubt, skepticism, uncontrollable anger, anti-Christ, anti-anointing, devil worship, divination, false gifting, occultism, fear that deceives, spirits of error, confusion, lying, finger pointing, accusation, rebellion, strife, rejection, spiritual blindness, spiritual deafness, doctrinal error, hyper-spirituality, super religious, hyper-sensitivity, overly sensitive, touchy, spirit that mixes the holy with the profane, all perverse spirits, spirits of the New Age, spirits that maintain a form of godliness but deny the power thereof. Take a deep breath and cough them out. Go in Jesus' name.

In the name of Jesus, I command out of me: spirits of:

Hypocrisy, deceit, flattery, irritability, irrationality, pride, haughtiness, apprehension, agitation, dullness of comprehension, spirits that cause me to be defensive all the time, contention, mental confusion, spirits that hinder prayer, that hinder the move of the Holy Spirit, un-submissive, anti-submissive, spirits that pull me away from God, that resist God and godly people, spirits that cause me to be unteachable, argumentative, fear, dread, fretting, anxiousness, impatience. Take a deep breath and cough them out. Go in Jesus' name.

In the name of Jesus, I command out of me: spirits of:

Control, suppressed anger, rage, resentment, unforgiveness, hate, self hate, bitterness, root of bitterness, spirits that cause me to wander from the truth, deception, chronic dissatisfaction, humiliation, mind binding, incoherence, forgetfulness, delusion, self delusion, and any spirit that manifest from my flesh. Go in Jesus' name. Take a deep breath and cough them out. Leave in Jesus' name.

Every demon and their kindred spirits that were called out leave me and enter me no more in Jesus' name.

Prayer of Thanksgiving

Thank you, Lord, for setting me free. Lord Jesus, I now ask you to come and bring the Holy Spirit to live in those areas where demons resided. I give You those places to reside and to rule and reign in them. Holy Spirit, give me wisdom and courage to change my lifestyle so that when the enemy tries to come back, he won't be able to. Amen!

Chapter 8
Repentance

The word repentance means reversal of decision. Repentance has a lot to do with the integrity of the heart and the willingness to forsake everything in order to follow Jesus Christ. In the following scripture, Christ symbolically illustrates the spiritual condition of one's heart using the example of the condition of the soil.

> "***Listen!*** *Behold, a sower went out to sow. And it happened, as he sowed, that some seed fell by the wayside; and the birds of the air came and devoured it. Some fell on* **stony ground**, *where it did not have much earth; and immediately it sprang up because it* **had no depth of earth**. *But when the sun was up it was scorched, and because it had no root it withered away.*
>
> *These likewise are the ones sown on stony ground who, when they hear the word, immediately receive it with gladness; and they have no root in themselves, and so endure only for a time. Afterward, when tribulation or persecution arises for the word's sake, immediately they stumble.* Mark 4:3-17 (NKJV)

In this parable, Jesus illustrates how the "Word" is not fruitful in the lives of many hearers, because their hearts are like stony ground. I have met many just like this whose repentance is only on the surface, very shallow.

There are two essentials with which to produce a good crop. (1.) fertile soil and (2.) depth of soil; otherwise the crop will die before reaching maturity and fruition.

Many times there is a willingness to hear the gospel and for a short while there might be a change in a person's life; but because there is *no depth of soil;* no depth of heart, it is a struggle for them to practice repentance when tribulation or trials arise and no depth of repentance to allow the necessary changes in the heart in order to grow into maturity.

Family, doing the right thing, the good thing, the Christ-like thing, when no one is looking is the fertilizer that builds up your soil. (Get my CD's on the "Demonic Nature of the Deeds of the Flesh and "Blocked Spiritual Growth.")

A rock is hard and unyielding. What does "s*tony ground* or *rocky soil*" represent in the Bible? It symbolizes hardened, unyielding, disobedience of the Word.

> *A new heart also will I give you, and a new spirit will I put within you: and I will take away the stony heart out of your flesh, and I will give you a heart of flesh.* Ezekiel 36:26 (KJV)

God desires to remove "*stony hearts*" from His children because it blocks obedience to Him and His Word. Many who claim to be followers of Christ have a superficial surrender to Him and wish to keep living life their own way out of their stony hearts, but James 1:21-27 (NKJV) instructs us:

> *Therefore lay aside all filthiness and overflow of wickedness, and receive with meekness the **implanted word**, which is able to save your souls.*

> *But be doers of the word, and not hearers only, deceiving yourselves. For if anyone is a hearer of the word and not a doer, he is like a man observing his natural face in a mirror; for he observes himself, goes away, and immediately forgets what kind of man he was. But he who looks into the perfect law of liberty and continues in it, and is not a forgetful hearer but a doer of the work, this one will be blessed in what he does.*

> *If anyone among you thinks he is religious, and does not bridle his tongue but deceives his own heart, this one's*

religion is useless. Pure and undefiled religion before God and the Father is this: to visit orphans and widows in their trouble, and to keep oneself unspotted from the world.

James is talking about the *implanted Word*. It means just that. The Word was planted in us. James is instructing us to RECEIVE the implanted Word. In order to receive, you have to accept it.

Shallow soil and stony ground means that there was a superficial acceptance of the Word. They received the Word initially and God's Word started to spring up and take root but as the roots went down into the soil, they hit rock. The rock prevented them from going any further. Soon the plant withered away.

What does this all mean? What was Jesus saying in this parable? He was saying that these people who heard the Word of God, had not made a complete repentance in their lives by removing all the rocks of sin that were present and hidden deep within their soul. They were not willing to make the sacrificial changes required in order to welcome and follow the words of Christ when trials, tribulation and the pressures of the world came. Thus their lives were scorched by the sun's heat because they had no root and withered away before becoming mature and fruitful – as happens to many Christians today.

As we can see from this, there is a surface repentance which brings people to Christ when they deal with their surface sins, and then there is a deeper repentance as they uncover their hard heartedness and deal with their sins that lie deeper under the top soil, which brings people into full maturity.

*Therefore, leaving the discussion of the elementary principles of Christ, let us go on to perfection, not laying again the **foundation of repentance** from dead works and of faith toward God, of the doctrine of baptisms, of* *laying on of hands, of resurrection of the dead, and of eternal judgment.* Hebrews 6:1-2 (NKJV)

Repentance is a foundation and a prerequisite to true salvation. All the Old Testament Prophets called for repentance. Starting with the New Testament, John the Baptist calls all to repent.

In those days John the Baptist came preaching in the wilderness of Judea, and saying, "Repent, for the kingdom of heaven is at hand!" Matthew 3:1-2 (NKJV)

In Matthew 4:17, we read the first message that Jesus preached was a call to repentance. *From that time Jesus began to preach and to say, "Repent, for the kingdom of heaven is at hand."* (KJV)

The first time that Jesus sent out His disciples, their message was repentance.

And He called the twelve to Himself, and began to send them out two by two, and gave them power over unclean spirits. He commanded them to take nothing for the journey except a staff
— no bag, no bread, no copper in their money belts —
but to wear sandals, and not to put on two tunics.

Also He said to them, "In whatever place you enter a house, stay there till you depart from that place. And whoever will not receive you nor hear you, when you depart from there, shake off the dust under your feet as a testimony against them. Assuredly, I say to you, it will be more tolerable for Sodom and Gomorrah in the day of judgment than for that city!"

So they went out and **preached that people should repent.**
Mark 6:7-12 (NKJV)

Jesus commissioned the entire church to preach repentance in order for people to receive forgiveness of sins and salvation.

*...and He said to them, "Thus it is written, that the Christ would suffer and rise again from the dead the third day, and that **repentance for forgiveness of sins** would be proclaimed in His name to all the nations, beginning from Jerusalem.* Luke 24:46-47 (NASB)

Who is speaking this here? It is Jesus Christ Himself. He plainly tells us here that repentance is the key to forgiveness of sins and the beginning of our Christian walk. The first message to the world after the death and resurrection of Jesus was spoken by the apostle Peter after the Holy Spirit filled the upper room. In Acts 2:37-38 we read:

*Now when they heard this, they were pierced to the heart, and said to Peter and the rest of the apostles, "Brethren, what shall we do?" Peter said to them, **"Repent,** and each of you be baptized in the name of Jesus Christ **for the forgiveness of your sins**; and you will receive the gift of the Holy Spirit.* (NASB)

That day, 3,000 were added to the group of believers. Peter later gave more detail to this call and said that a person must fully repent of all acts and attitudes of sin and turn to God in order to truly receive remission of the guilt and the penalty of sin and receive Christ into his heart.

*"Therefore **repent and return, so that your sins may be wiped away,** in order that times of refreshing may come from the presence of the Lord; and that He may send Jesus, the Christ appointed for you,* Acts 3:19-20 (NASB)

Peter declared that a person must fully repent of ALL acts and attitudes of sin and turn to God in order to fully receive remission of guilt and penalty of sin and receive Jesus Christ in his heart. There is simply NO salvation or refreshing without repentance.

So, what then is repentance? The word repent in the Webster's dictionary mean to change one's ways because of contrition. In other words, it means to have a change of mind which results in a decision to turn from going in one direction, turn around and go in the opposite direction. Repentance is not only a desire, emotion, or intention to turn but it is **the act of turning**. Therefore, repentance starts in a thought and becomes a deed.

Repentance is not what you intend to do, for it is not REAL repentance until you have done it. Repentance is not like making a New Year's resolution, but instead it is an act of turning away from every form and appearance of evil and turning to God. It is an act of walking in God's ways.

*And you He made alive, who were dead in trespasses and sins, in which **you once walked** according to the course of this world, according to the prince of the power of the air, the spirit who now works in the sons of disobedience* Ephesians 2:1-2 (NKJV)

Repentance is not remorse. Remorse, no matter how intense and sincere is only an emotion. True repentance is remorse with a definite and deliberate and decisive deed. Remorse is something you feel. Repentance is something you do.

Many people feel remorseful for misconduct or deeds or sins that they have committed, but that remorse does not always cause them to repent and cease from engaging in that wrongful conduct. The apostle Paul addresses this in 2 Corinthians 7:9-11

Now I rejoice, not that you were made sorry, but that your sorrow led to repentance. For you were made sorry in a godly manner, that you might suffer loss from us in nothing. For godly sorrow produces repentance leading to salvation, not to be regretted; but the sorrow of the world produces death. For observe this very thing, that you sorrowed in a godly manner: What diligence it produced in you, what clearing of yourselves, what indignation, what fear, what vehement desire, what zeal, what vindication! In all things you proved yourselves to be clear in this matter. (NKJV)

Paul is very pleased that their sorrow led to repentance and into salvation and thus cleansed them. In his letter to the Corinthians, Paul goes much further in how he feels about those in the church (so-called brothers and sisters) who continue to live their lives unrepented.

Immorality and sin must be judged.

It is actually reported that there is sexual immorality among you, and such sexual immorality as is not even named among the Gentiles—that a man has his father's wife! And you are puffed up, and have not rather mourned, that he who has done this deed might be taken away from among you. For I indeed, as absent in body but present in spirit, have already judged (as though I were present) him who has so done this deed.

In the name of our Lord Jesus Christ, when you are gathered together, along with my spirit, with the power of our Lord Jesus Christ, deliver such a one to Satan for the destruction of the flesh, that his spirit may be saved in the day of the Lord Jesus.

Your glorying is not good. Do you not know that a little leaven leavens the whole lump? Therefore purge out the old leaven, that you may be a new lump, since you truly are unleavened. For indeed Christ, our Passover, was sacrificed for us. Therefore let us keep the feast, not with old leaven, nor with the leaven of malice and wickedness, but with the unleavened bread of sincerity and truth.

I wrote to you in my epistle not to keep company with sexually immoral people. Yet I certainly did not mean with the sexually immoral people of this world, or with the covetous, or extortioners, or idolaters, since then you would need to go out of the world. But now I have written to you not to keep company with anyone named a brother, who is sexually immoral, or covetous, or an idolater, or a reviler, or a drunkard, or an extortioner— not even to eat with such a person.

For what have I to do with judging those also who are outside? Do you not judge those who are inside? But those who are outside God judges. Therefore ***"put away from yourselves the evil person."*** 1 Corinthians 5:1-13 (NKJV)

Paul urges us to examine ourselves in 2 Corinthians 13:5 (NKJV).

Examine yourselves as to whether you are in the faith. Test yourselves. Do you not know yourselves, that Jesus Christ is in you?—unless indeed you are disqualified.

Paul also tells us that we have become a new creation in Christ.

Therefore, if anyone is in Christ, he is a new creation; old things have passed away; behold, all things have become new. 2 Corinthians 5:17 (NKJV). In other words, there is a changed life when you come to Christ. In order for repentance to have validity, there must be an inward repentance for an outward repentance to take place. Let us look at inward repentance in Psalm 51:6:

Behold, You desire truth in the inward parts, And in the hidden
part *You will make me to know wisdom.* (NKJV)

All sin is of the heart; the inward part of man, the innermost being. It can be defined as an inward attitude of rebellion. Sin is described as an attitude or an act of rebellion against God's law. It is disobedience of God's word. It breaches the fellowship with God and defiles the offender. Before sin finds an outward way to express, it first begins in the heart in the form of a rebellious attitude.

Jesus told us about the inward part of man, the heart, in:

Matthew 15:18-20 (NKJV)

> *But those things which proceed out of the mouth come from the heart, and they defile a man. For out of the heart proceed evil thoughts, murders, adulteries, fornications, thefts, false witness, blasphemies. These are the things which defile a man,*

Jesus describes the inward attitude as the heart of man. It is the inward attitudes that we must first repent of in order to make a complete surrender to God. We must go beyond the superficial repentance to the hidden part, the inward man for this process of repentance to be effective. We try to fool ourselves, but we can't fool God.

> *And there is no creature hidden from His sight, but all things are naked and open to the eyes of Him to whom we must give account.* Hebrews 4:13 (NKJV)

God requires that we turn away from serving Satan and instead serve Him. He also requires us to turn away from sin and turn towards purity and holiness.

> *Draw near to God and He will draw near to you, Cleanse your hands, you sinners; and purify your hearts, you double-minded.* James 4:8 (NASB)

Our walk with God must not include sin, but should require us to put away sin. It is a walk of holiness. Holy behavior can only come from a changed inward life.

> *As obedient children, do not be conformed to the former lusts which were yours in your ignorance, but like the Holy One who called you, be holy yourselves also in all your behavior; because it is written, "YOU SHALL BE HOLY, FOR I AM HOLY."* 1 Peter 1:14-16 (NASB)

Make no mistake about it. If anyone does not obey Jesus Christ through obeying God's word, he has not entered communion and fellowship with Him and anyone who says he knows God but does not obey His commandments and live a Holy life, God calls him an outright liar.

> *Now by this we know that we know Him, if we keep His commandments. He who says, "I know Him," and does not keep His commandments, is a liar, and the truth is not in him. But whoever keeps His word, truly the love of God is perfected in him. By this we know that we are in Him. He who says he abides in Him ought himself also to walk just as He walked.* 1 John 2:3-6 (NKJV)

Jesus makes it clear in John's gospel that anyone who does not obey God's commandments does not know Him nor love Him:

> *"If you love Me, keep My commandments.* John 14:15 (NKJV)

> *He who has My commandments and keeps them, it is he who loves Me. And he who loves Me will be loved by My Father, and I will love him and manifest Myself to him."* John 14:21 (NKJV)

> *Jesus answered and said to him, "If anyone loves Me, he will keep My word; and My Father will love him, and We will come to him and make Our home with him. He who does not love Me does not keep My words; and the word which you hear is not Mine but the Father's who sent Me.* John 14:23-24 (NKJV)

These are the things that should happen if you have truly repented.

1. You will Love God and Love People

> *Jesus said to him, "'You shall love the LORD your God with all your heart, with all your soul, and with all your mind.' This is the first and great commandment. And the second is like it: 'You shall love your neighbor as yourself.'"* Matthew 22:37-39 (NKJV)

2. People will see your goodness and good fruit you produce

But the fruit of the Spirit is love, joy, peace, patience, kindness, goodness, faithfulness, gentleness, self-control; Galatians 5:22- 23 (NASB)

3. You will know them by their fruits

Do men gather grapes from thorn bushes or figs from thistles? Even so, every good tree bears good fruit, but a bad tree bears bad fruit. A good tree cannot bear bad fruit, nor can a bad tree bear good fruit. Every tree that does not bear good fruit is cut down and thrown into the fire. Therefore by their fruits you will know them. Matthew 7:16-20 (NKJV)

4. And the Lord will see that you are not practicing of sins so that He would not declare that he never knew you.

"Not everyone who says to Me, 'Lord, Lord,' shall enter the kingdom of heaven, but he who does the will of My Father in heaven. Many will say to Me in that day, 'Lord, Lord, have we not prophesied in Your name, cast out demons in Your name, and done many wonders in Your name?' And then I will declare to them, 'I never knew you; depart from Me, you who practice lawlessness!'"

"Therefore whoever hears these sayings of Mine, and does them, I will liken him to a wise man who built his house on the rock... Matthew 7:21-24 (NKJV)

5. A Love for the Brethren

Beloved, let us love one another, for love is of God; and everyone who loves is born of God and knows God. He who does not love does not know God, for God is love. 1 John 4:7-8 (NKJV)

In this the children of God and the children of the devil are manifest: Whoever does not practice righteousness is not of God, nor is he who does not love his brother.

For this is the message that you heard from the beginning, that we should love one another, not as Cain who was of the wicked one and murdered his brother. And why did he murder him? Because his works were evil and his brother's righteous.

Do not marvel, my brethren, if the world hates you. We know that we have passed from death to life, because we love the brethren. He who does not love his brother abides in death. 1 John 3:10-14 (NKJV)

6. A person who has repented has a hatred for the ways of the world.

Adulterers and adulteresses! Do you not know that friendship with the world is enmity with God? Whoever therefore wants to be a friend of the world makes himself an enemy of God. James 4:4 (NKJV)

7. A person who has repented has an overcoming life

For whatever is born of God overcomes the world. And this is the victory that has overcome the world—our faith. 1 John 5:4 (NKJV)

8. A person who has repented has a new heart

I will give you a new heart and put a new spirit within you; I will take the heart of stone out of your flesh and give you a heart of flesh. Ezekiel 36:26 (NKJV)

9. A person who has repented is obedient to the word of God

Jesus said: *"If you love Me, keep My commandments.* John 14:15 (NKJV)

10. A person who has repented is a slave to righteousness

Likewise you also, reckon yourselves to be dead indeed to sin, but alive to God in Christ Jesus our Lord.

Therefore do not let sin reign in your mortal body, that you should obey it in its lusts. And do not present your members as instruments of unrighteousness to sin, but present yourselves to God as being alive from the dead, and your members as instruments of righteousness to God. For sin shall not have dominion over you, for you are not under law but under grace.

What then? Shall we sin because we are not under law but under grace? Certainly not! Do you not know that to whom you present yourselves slaves to obey, you are that one's slaves whom you obey, whether of sin leading to death, or of obedience leading to righteousness? But God be thanked that though you were slaves of sin, yet you obeyed from the heart that form of doctrine to which you were delivered. And having been set free from sin, you became slaves of righteousness. Romans 6:11-18 (NKJV)

Family, we are no longer slaves of sin but now we submit to be slaves of God, doing His will and not our own anymore. And those are the key points of living a repentant life.

Next, we are going to cast out all unclean, evil, demonic spirits that have afflicted you, harassed you, and influenced you. They come out in the name of Jesus and they come out in the breath.

When Jesus cast them out, they came out in a loud voice. There is a lot of breath that is expelled in order to make a loud voice. An interesting thing is that in the "Vines Complete Expository Dictionary" the Greek word for spirit and breath is the same word. ("pneuma"). When Jesus was casting out spirits a lot of "pneuma was expelled, that is breath/spirit. So in this deliverance, as a act of your will, I will ask you to blow out breath in the name of Jesus to start the process of (evil) "spirits" leaving.

As you go through deliverance, speak aloud as you command out the spirits.

In the name of Jesus Christ, I command out of me all spirits that are hostile toward God:

Adultery, fornication, uncleanness, lewdness, idolatry, sorcery, hatred, contentions, outbursts of anger, selfish ambitions, dissensions, heresies, envy, murders, drunkenness, revelries. Go in Jesus' name. (Blow out breath). Leave in Jesus' name.

In the name of Jesus, I command out of me:

Evil thoughts, adulteries, fornications, thefts, covetousness, greed, wickedness, deceit, lewdness, spirit of the evil eye, blasphemy, pride, foolishness, spirit of slavery and bondage, bitterness, spirits that are attached to iniquity, transgression and sins, spirit of offense, rejection, anger and pride by being insulted, a racist spirit of intolerance, bigotry, prejudice, spite, and hatred towards another nationality, lust of deceit, condemnation self-condemnation, guilt, shame, misrepresentation, falsehood, intentional fraud, betrayal, double dealing, trickery, insecurity, misleading, cheat, spirit that makes me CRAVE, (name your CRAVING……..), uncleanness, passion for evil desire, and covetousness, idolatry. disobedience, unthankful, ungrateful, selfishness, pride of life. Go in Jesus' name. (Blow out breath). Leave in Jesus' name.

In the name of Jesus, I command out of me:

Rejection, envy, jealousy, suspicion, paranoia, anger, deception, murder, fear, control, witchcraft, accusation, perverseness, self pity, pouting, bitterness, resentment, false compassion, compulsive behavior, self accusations, deception, lying, possessiveness, rebellion, divination, division, divorce, depression, discouragement, despair, hopelessness, suicide, vanity, scorner, scoffer, sexually dysfunctional, torment, terror, fantasy, self hate, perfection, acute anxiety, panic disorder, chronic anxiety, hyperventilation syndrome, bondage, egotism, intolerance, frustration, death. Go in Jesus' name. (Blow out breath). Leave in Jesus' name.

In the name of Jesus, I command out of me:

Violence, unteachable, gluttony, alcoholism, shame, religious spirits, fear of man, selfishness, distrust, sociopath, psychopath, lust of the world, dysfunctional, addicted to sports, addicted to movies, addicted to books, addicted to the internet, no sex drive, rape, unclean thoughts, vain imaginations, escape, lust for power- for position-for money, arrested development in spiritual growth, in mental growth, in emotional growth, in physical growth, seduction, sexual lust, bulimia, anorexia, nymphomania, gigolo, whoremonger, sexual abuse, child abuse, rape, child molestation, sarcasm, narcissus, hate, fornication, poverty, dyslexia. Go in Jesus' name. (Blow out breath). Leave in Jesus' name.

In the name of Jesus, I command out of me:

Bestiality, incest, stubbornness, disrespect, machismo, greed, self worship, lust for material things, addiction to shopping, drugs, food, gossip, miser, penny pinching, hoarding, accumulation, pack rat, homosexuality, mind control, condemnation, bondage in abusive relationships, cannot accept responsibility, failure, vagabond, insecurity, phobias to germs, to crowds, fear of the dark, memory problems, fatigue, bitterness, slumber, tiredness, sleeping all the time, nit picking, perfection, vanity, critical spirit, Obsessive Compulsive behavior, checking, re-checking, obsessive planner, obsessive cleaner, obsessive counting, re-counting, self hatred, false responsibility, resisting, foot dragging, punishment using time schedules, punishment using sex, punishment using rejection, intolerance, conceit, projection of blame anti-Christ, legalism, spirits that cause confusion, inability to concentrate, decreased attention span, memory loss, cloudy thinking, drowsiness, headaches. Go in Jesus' name. (Blow out breath0. Leave in

Jesus' name.

In the name of Jesus, I command out of me:

Rejection, abandonment, failure, negativity, pessimism, judgmental, opposition, condemnation, guilt, criticism, betrayal, fear of commitment, fear of responsibility, fear of authority, fear of diseases, fear of darkness, fear of being alone, fear of death. fear of being closed in, fear of a sound, fear of foods, fear of certain words, (Name your own fears….). Go in Jesus' name. (Blow out breath). Leave in Jesus' name.

In the name of Jesus, I command out of me:

Selfishness, superiority, controlling, vanity, overbearing, boastful, rebellious, conceited, selfish ambition, rudeness, man-pleaser, insolent, always right, insensitive, presumptuous, arrogant, self love, self righteous, spirit that wants attention, haughty, self interest, unloving, self glory, egotistical, I, I, I, ME, ME, ME, Spirit, possessiveness, Go in Jesus' name. (Blow out breath). Leave in Jesus' name.

In Jesus' name, I command out of me:

Punishment, discontentment, dishonor to self, to others, fear of loosing honor, fear of being punished, hopelessness, helplessness, humiliation, put down, ridicule, failure, stupid thinking, stupid decisions, senseless mind, foolishness, lack of knowledge, lack of wisdom. Go in Jesus' name. (Blow out breath). Leave in Jesus' name.

In Jesus' name, I command out of me:

Sexual idolatry, homosexuality, greed, troubled heart, poverty of spirit, poverty of soul, poverty of the body, lack, insufficiency, pride, trouble receiving, trouble maker, attention seeking, callousness, hard hearted, cruelty, revenge, cold love, cold shoulder, punishing others, ungratefulness, false front, denial, stealing, lying, dishonesty, stretching the truth, craftiness, schemer, always controlling and maneuvering others. Go in Jesus' name. (Blow out breath). Leave in Jesus' name.

In Jesus name, I command out of me:

Rudeness, traitor, cowardice, turmoil, muddled mind, forgetfulness, superiority, depression, flashbacks, painful thoughts, escape, hysteria, losing control, withdrawal, nervousness, loss of concentration, sloppiness, temper, irritation, hostility, bitter love, self centeredness. Go in Jesus' name. (Blow out breath). Leave in Jesus' name.

In Jesus' name, I command out of me:

Addiction, addictiveness, bad habits, ungodly compulsions and cravings, slavery or bondage to sin, procrastination, nervousness stress, tension, distrust, unreliability, fear of looking stupid, self hate for wrong decisions, abuse, self abuse, emotional abuse, mental abuse, physical abuse, sexual abuse, anger, Go in Jesus' name. (Blow out breath). Leave in Jesus' name.

In Jesus' name, I command out of me:

Guilt, rage, out of control anger, pain, sickness, compromise, intellectualism, egotism, bragging, pride, automatic response, accident prone, self destruction, all spirits of pride, defiance, haughtiness, self-righteousness, criticism, judgmental, murmuring, grumbling, complaining, rebellion, contention, fighting, competition, vanity, self worship, arrogance, insolence, discontent, doctorial, egotism, bragging, mockery, self accession, self-promotion, exaggeration, flattery, lover of power, perfectionism, stubbornness, anger, rage, temper, violence, murder, and the source of all these demons to leave me now in Jesus' name. Take a deep breath and cough them out. Go in Jesus' name.

In the name of Jesus Christ, I command out of me: every

Anti-Christ spirit, anti-God spirit, every spirit that rejects God, the bride of Satan, vampirism, blood drinking, the prince of darkness. Take a deep breath and cough them out. Go in Jesus' name.

In the name of Jesus Christ, I command out of me:

All spirits of rejection, fear of being rejected, self rejection, spirits that make me feel unloved, unwanted, not needed, insecurity, inferiority, and all like spirits leave me now. Take a deep breath and cough them out. Go in Jesus' name.

In the name of Jesus Christ, I command out of me spirits of:

Loneliness, depression, lost hope, despair, self pity, despondency, desperation, discouragement, hopelessness, isolation, spirits that make me feel like pulling back, pulling out, giving up, defeated, sunkeness, dullness, flattened, let down, criminal minded, wrong thinking, insanity, madness, suicide, spirit of death. Take a deep breath and cough them out. Go in Jesus' name.

In the name of Jesus Christ, I command out of me all spirits of:

Lying, spirits of error, lust of the eyes, pride of life, self love, narcissism, self-righteousness, spirits that puff up, show off, braggart, boastful, egotistical, haughty, high-minded, vanity, show- off, cursing, blasphemy, and all like spirits. Take a deep breath and cough them out. Go in Jesus' name.

In the name of Jesus Christ, I command out of me all evil spirits of:

Delusion, delirium, delusional disorder, illusion, paranoia, hallucinations, schizophrenia, bipolar disorder, distress, disturbed mind, betrayed reasoning, covetousness, foolishness, folly, ambition greed, self worship, idolatry, self deception, self delusion, selfish desires, fixed misconceptions, fixed false beliefs. Take a deep breath and cough them out. Go in Jesus' name.

In the name of Jesus, I command out of me all spirits of

Religious error, every spirit of defeatism, witchcraft, unbelief, doubt, skepticism, uncontrollable anger, anti-Christ, anti-anointing, devil worship, divination, false gifting, occultism, fear that deceives, spirits of error, confusion, lying, finger pointing, accusation, rebellion strife, rejection, spiritual blindness, spiritual deafness, doctrinal error, hyper spirituality, super religious, hyper sensitivity, overly sensitive, touchy, spirit that mixes the holy with the profane, all perverse spirits, spirits of the New Age, spirits that maintain a form of godliness but deny the power thereof. Take a deep breath and cough them out. Go in Jesus' name.

In the name of Jesus, I command out of me spirits of:

Hypocrisy, deceit, flattery, irritability, irrationality, pride, haughtiness, apprehension, agitation, dullness of comprehension, spirits that cause me to be defensive all the time, contention, mental confusion, spirits that hinder prayer, that hinder the move of the Holy Spirit, un-submissive, anti-submissive, spirits that pull me away from God, that resist God and godly people, spirits that cause me to be unteachable, argumentative, fear, dread, fretting, anxiousness, impatience. Take a deep breath and cough them out. Go in Jesus' name.

In the name of Jesus, I command out of me spirits of:

Control, suppressed anger, rage, resentment, unforgiveness, hate, self hatred, bitterness, root of bitterness, spirits that cause me to wander from the truth, deception, chronic dissatisfaction, humiliation, mind binding, incoherence, forgetfulness, delusion, self delusion, and any evil spirit that manifest from my flesh. Go in Jesus' name. Take a deep breath and cough them out. Go in Jesus' name.

I speak in Jesus' name to every demon and their kindred spirits that were called out – leave me and enter me no more.

Thank you, Lord Jesus, for setting me free. Lord, I now ask you to come and bring the Holy Spirit to live in those areas where demons resided. I give You those places to reside and to rule and reign in. Holy Spirit, give me wisdom and courage to change my lifestyle so that when the enemy tries to come back, he won't be able to. Amen!

Chapter 9
Self Deliverance

One day I watched as my wife got out the broom and started to knock down the spider webs on our screened patio when we lived in Cooper city, Florida. They were a real nuisance when trying to walk around on our pool deck. We would find that we were always getting them stuck on us and would have to brush them off. So, Jill went out there with a broom periodically to sweep them down. Then one day, I noticed that she took it a step further. She started putting the spiders in the pool to kill them. At first she was just knocking down the webs and then she attacked the source of the webs, the spiders.

Many of us spend years of our lives just knocking down the web without really addressing the source of the web. We go through life suffering physical emotional and spiritual failure because we just knock down the webs. The problem is not the web so much as it is the spider. Suffering and failure, whether spiritual or physical, is not sin, but the consequence of sin. We cannot get rid of sin by merely dealing with each sin, we must get rid of the root cause of sin. You will never eliminate the spider webs just by them knocking them down, you must catch the spider and eliminate it's activity from your territory – your life.

John the Baptist said in, Matthew 3:10 (NKJV) *And even now the ax is laid to the root of the trees. Therefore every tree which does not bear good fruit is cut down and thrown into the fire.*

If we are to be successful in deliverance, we must lay an ax to the root of the problem. If sin is only the *spider web*, then what is the *spider*? How do we eliminate it? Deliverance from demons is a good start at knocking down the webs, but the ultimate goal is to get to the spider, the cause of the web. If not, the web seems to reappear.

When counseling with people, my objective is to uncover their true motives and the source of their motives, which is at the root of the problem. I let them talk about their lives. They talk about what wounded them, hurt them, offended them, and those things produced attitudes that they now express in their lives. I found out a long time ago that whatever is in you will at some point come out of you in an expression of attitude. So I probe and try to find where the wounds are and if you listen long enough, you will find the real reason, the real cause of the demonic activity.

Many times, they have been rejected in life. I find that when you break it all down you will find a lot of people have been rejected in one way or another.

When working in deliverance, it is important to listen to the Holy Spirit. As demons are being called out, the Holy Spirit often reveals the source of that demon to the minister or to the one being ministered to. If you get a picture of how that demon came into your life or a word or a picture in your mind of the source of that demonic activity in your life then those demons should be called out along with the original one being called out.

For example, if you are calling out the spirit of lust and you get an impression of an incident, such as a rape or molestation or you may get an impression of pornography through magazines or movies when they were picked up and watched, then you need to call out those evil spirits that came in when those things happened.

Or you may get the impression of something that does not have to do with sex or lust such as, the impression of rejection from a mother or a father, or an impression of violence. Then take that impression that the Holy Spirit gives you even though it has nothing to do with sex or lust and call out the spirit of rejection or violence or any other impression or word that the Holy Spirit gives you. Such as, "You, evil spirit, the one that came into me/him when I saw or when I was abused, or when that incident happened (and you name the incident....). Come out of me in the name of Jesus! You see, Family, God has revealed through a Holy Spirit snap-shot in your mind of the entrance point of that demon. God has revealed the source or the root or the spider of the web so to speak.

If you are tired of being a slave to whatever controls you, then it is time to get to the root of it and lay the ax to the root of the tree. Amen? As you are getting to the source of the problems, the Holy Spirit reveals pictures in your mind leading you back to the root source. The root problem reveals what enslaves.

At the end of this section, we will do deliverance. When we get to that part, have a pencil and some paper ready to write down the word that seems to hit your button, and off to the side of it, the impression that you get from that word and you will get to the source of that demon. It may be a name, a place, or the face of a person that was responsible for the demon to enter into your life.

No amount of deliverance can replace the central need in a person's life to accept the Lordship of Jesus, and to live out the reality of that commitment. Often, I see people having to go over the same ground again and again. One reason is that they are not trying to live out their commitment with Jesus in the place where they just got delivered, so they battle the same ground over and over. This is why they repeat the same problem after they've been set free.

It is so important to live out your commitment to Jesus Christ in concrete terms for Him to have Lordship every part of your life and especially in the place where those demons used to be. For permanent deliverance, a person must commit to have Jesus rule and reign in the area where demonic activity used to rule and reign. Otherwise deliverance is useless.

The Bible has a warning about demons who were once cast out and are allowed to come back in and dwell in the same person.

*"When an unclean spirit goes out of a man, he goes through dry places, seeking rest, and finds none. Then he says, 'I will **return to my house** from which I came.' And when he comes, he finds it empty, swept, and put in order. Then he goes and takes with him seven other spirits more wicked than himself, and they enter and dwell there; and the last state of that man is worse than the first. So shall it also be with this wicked generation."* Matthew 12:34-45 (NKJV)

Notice the demon called it **"his house"** and next, he finds it **unoccupied swept and put in order.** When a person receives deliverance, their spiritual house is swept and put in order. I want you also to notice that the demon first finds it unoccupied. Deliverance has cleaned it out. Deliverance has swept it and put it in order. Then, the demon that was cast out looks into the person and sees there has been no change, for he finds it empty unoccupied. And then, as it says in verse 45, *Then he goes and takes with him seven other spirits more wicked than himself, and they enter and dwell there; and the last state of that man is worse than the first.*

I have met many who have gone through deliverance who refused to let Jesus rule and reign in their life after their deliverance. They refused to let him have access to those areas in their lives where demons used to rule and reign, and because they refused to change their life-style, those demons that were cast out came back bringing seven more deadly than themselves and the last date was worse than the first state.

Do you remember the incident at the pool of Bethesda when Jesus asked the man, do you wish to be healed?

(John.5:1-15) The price for freedom and deliverance is that you first wish to be healed and next you take a stand against the enemy with Jesus ruling and reigning in the area where those demons used to rule and reign. But it is up to you. When you make a commitment to be set free in deliverance, you are responsible for the retention of your healing and deliverance once you have been set free. This is why it is so important to have Jesus reign in concrete terms where the demons use to reign. Not only that, but don't go back to that demonic practice. Don't let him in, or your last state becomes worst than the former state.

Here is an example of what I mean. Let's say, you are addicted to drugs and you just received deliverance from the spirit of addiction (sorcery) and you were set free. Then you go to your medicine cabinet and open the door and there is the prescription bottle of the pills that you were addicted to. It is right then and there at that point that you must decide take a stand against the enemy and let Jesus rule and reign in the area of your addiction. This is a place where you are being tested. You may say to yourself, "I can just take one pill" and the other voice inside of you is saying, "Take a stand in Jesus." This is where the battle rages. If you wish to be healed you must take a stand in Jesus or else your addiction will come back with other demons attached to it.

Deliverance is a gift which helps man and woman live an aggressive and effective Christian life. Deliverance belongs to God's children. In Matthew 15:27 Jesus declares that deliverance is the children's bread.

In Matthew 12:28, Jesus told the Pharisees, *"but if I cast out demons by the spirit of God, then the kingdom of God has come upon you."* Deliverance from demons is the kingdom of God coming upon you by the Holy Spirit, the spirit of God. It is the kingdom of God coming against the Kingdom of Satan who has found homes inside of men, women and children. A major part of Jesus' public ministry was to cast out demons. In various places in the New

Testament, we find demons crying out of people at the presence of Jesus.

Demons cried out of a man and said, "What business do we have with each other, Jesus of Nazareth? Have you come to destroy us? I know who you are, the Holy One of God." Mark 1:24 (NASB)

Wherever Jesus went he healed many who were ill with various diseases, and cast out many demons (Mark 1:34). In doing so, he was announcing the downfall of Satan's kingdom. From that time until now, the kingdom of God has come upon the world in the ministries of Christ, but none is more noticed than the deliverance ministry.

Satan has a strategy to keep men in bondage to sin and to the world thus keeping them from the kingdom of God entirely and rendering ineffective those who are already in God's kingdom.

Nothing destroys the testimony of a Christian faster than one who is bound to any form of demonic activity. Do you know what I mean? Many Christians give Jesus a black eye by what they do or say, because of demons who live in their flesh or soul. Their testimony is rendered ineffective because their lives are contrary to Christ's life, and they need to be set free from demons in order to be good representatives of Jesus Christ.

Therefore those who were scattered went everywhere preaching the word. Then Philip went down to the city of Samaria and preached Christ to them. And the multitudes with one accord heeded the things spoken by Philip, hearing and seeing the miracles which he did. For unclean spirits, crying with a loud voice, came out of many who were possessed; and many who were paralyzed and lame were healed. And there was great joy in that city.

But there was a certain man called Simon, who previously practiced sorcery in the city and astonished the people of Samaria, claiming that he was someone great, to whom they all gave heed, from the least to the greatest, saying, "This man is the great power of God." And they heeded him because he had astonished them with his sorceries for a long time. But when they believed Philip as he preached the things concerning the kingdom of God and the name of Jesus Christ, both men and women were baptized. Then Simon himself also believed; and when he was baptized he continued with Philip, and was amazed, seeing the miracles and signs which were done.

Now when the apostles who were at Jerusalem heard that Samaria had received the word of God, they sent Peter and John to them, who, when they had come down, prayed for them that they might receive the Holy Spirit. For as yet He had fallen upon none of them. They had only been baptized in the name of the Lord Jesus. Then they laid hands on them, and they received the Holy Spirit.

And when Simon saw that through the laying on of the apostles' hands the Holy Spirit was given, he offered them money saying, "Give me this power also, that anyone on whom I lay hands may receive the Holy Spirit."

*But Peter said to him, "Your money perish with you, because you thought that the gift of God could be purchased with money! You have neither part nor portion in this matter, **for your heart is not right in the sight of God**. Repent therefore of this **your wickedness**, and pray God if perhaps the thought of your heart may be forgiven you. For I see that you are **poisoned by bitterness and bound by iniquity**."*

Then Simon answered and said, "Pray to the Lord for me, that none of the things which you have spoken may come upon me." Acts 8:4-24 (NKJV)

This passage clearly shows us and that some people, who respond to the gospel of the kingdom of God; the good news that God loves them and provides a way for them to go to heaven, may have been baptized, may follow the teachings of Jesus, but still need deliverance. They still have demons that need to be dealt with. This does not mean they are not Christians; it means that some of them may still need deliverance.

Paul writes to us and warns believers that some false teachers will come and lead them astray, corrupting their minds.

*But I fear, lest somehow, as the serpent deceived Eve by his craftiness, so your minds may be corrupted from the simplicity that is in Christ. For if he who comes preaches **another Jesus** whom we have not preached, or if you receive **a different spirit** which you have not received, or **a different gospel** which you have not accepted—you may well put up with it!* 2 Corinthians 11:3-4 (NKJV)

Paul warns us that these false teachers will come and turn people away from the simple gospel of Jesus Christ and mix in other teachings to make *"another Jesus,"* a *different gospel* and in the process will receive a *different spirit*. And it is not the same Jesus and the same gospel that Paul preached. Just like Satan, who deceived Eve by his clever lies, Paul warns us that false teachers will come with their clever lies to lead people into a different gospel, another Jesus, and receive a different spirit. And he warns us that we will put up with it – in other words, we will tolerate it.

When we receive their teachings, we receive another spirit and embrace a different gospel. They may teach the gospel of transcendental meditation, or yoga and the gospel of Jesus, forming another gospel and another Jesus. Their gospel may be all about the love of "God," receiving the best of everything, cars, jobs, houses, like a Santa Claus father-god- who brings good gifts, but they never bring the full biblical Jesus. Yes, the gospel of Jesus is about love and forgiveness, but the full gospel of Jesus includes all that Jesus did on the cross to save mankind from hell. It includes repentance, holiness, obedience and victory from sin and that needs to be preached also.

So, when we cast out the spirit of false doctrines and false teachers, we must cast out the spirit of the false gospel, false Jesus, and the different spirit that we received when we believed them.

*Finally, my brethren, be strong in the Lord and in the power of His might. Put on the whole armor of God, that you may be able to **stand against** the wiles of the devil. For we do not wrestle against flesh and blood, but against principalities, against powers, against the rulers of the darkness of this age, against spiritual hosts of wickedness in the heavenly places. Therefore take up the whole armor of God, that you may be able to **withstand** in the evil day, and having done all, to stand.*

***Stand therefore**, having girded your waist with truth, having put on the breastplate of righteousness, and having shod your feet with the preparation of the gospel of peace; above all, taking the shield of faith with which you will be able to quench all the fiery darts of the wicked one. And take the helmet of salvation, and the sword of the Spirit, which is the word of God; praying always with all prayer and supplication in the Spirit, being watchful to this end with all perseverance and supplication for all the saints.* Ephesians 6:10-8 (NKJV)

In these verses, we are told to stand several times. When you resist the devil you need to stand and stand firm against those things that are being cast out of you.

James 4:7 (NKJV) says: *Therefore submit to God. Resist the devil and he will flee from you.* If you have resisted the devil, but you have not submitted to God, you haven't really taken a stand. Many times, people phone me for deliverance, but they themselves have not taken a stand against the devil by submitting to God. They want me to resist the devil for them in the power of my strength without them submitting to God. They just want me to do it for them.

In order to receive and keep your deliverance, you must change your mind and be tired of being in sin, sick and want to be set free. You must submit to God and take a stand against the devil. Some people don't mind the condition that they are in. They have gotten used to it. They have found comfort in their condition. People help them and they get sympathy, so why should they take a stand against it?

We read in John 5:14 that after Jesus healed the man at the pool of Bethesda he found the man in the Temple and he said to him a very profound thing. He said, *"behold you have become well, do not sin anymore, so that nothing worse happens to you."* It is here that we see that in this man's case Jesus tied his sin to his disease and sickness. This man was told to go and sin no more another words, take a stand.

Once, a man with an alcohol problem he could not overcome came to me for deliverance. After much deliverance he said, "Why can't I just be a happy drunk like I used to be? He really didn't want full deliverance, just partial deliverance of his problem and not the source of his problem. That would require his taking a stand to obey God.

Another time, I ministered to a woman who wanted all her spiritual problems solved but then asked me not to cast out the spirit of nicotine. She was addicted to that spirit and did not want to take a stand against it. The demon gave her comfort. I was going to the root of the problem but she did not want to be completely healed.

Some time ago, I began praying for someone who was wearing a neck collar because of an automobile accident. I began to pray for her neck to be healed but she stopped me, and said, "No, no, don't pray for my neck; pray for my insurance claim." Some people have ulterior motives for why they don't want to be healed. All I could pray was "Let Your will be done, Lord."

Now, when trying to recognize whether or not there is an evil spirit attached to you or someone else, we must look at several things. Some of these things are if our old nature refuses to stay dead or that vicious temper remains untamed, that unwholesome or shameful appetite still demands satisfaction, fear, anxiety continues to weaken you, or anything that compels you, controls you, or drives you into sin.

If these things are happening to you or someone else, there is a strong indication that evil spirits have managed to invade your personality, taking dominion and control from within you. In Matthew 8:28-32 we are told a story of the insane man in the tombs screaming and cutting himself. When Jesus approached the man, the demons in that man revealed that they have a will. They spoke out, "If you are going to cast us out, send us into the herd of swine." They showed they have a preference and a will.

That is why I lead you to say, "I command out of me," when we are doing deliverance. It is placing your will for deliverance against the will of the demons. When you command them out of you in the name of Jesus, you are putting your own will to work against those evil spirits.

I have had to shift to this tactic many times when commanding out an evil spirit and it speaks out of the person, "I won't go, she enjoys me, she wants me to stay, I have a right to stay, or I live here." When a person does not will to be set free, they give that demon legal right to remain. That is why I have the person put their own will behind the deliverance. It is then that the evil spirit is dislodged from them and cast out.

I have encountered people who could not give themselves self deliverance because an evil spirit was blocking their deliverance. A young woman called me on the telephone. She had played an occult game called, "Mary Worth." She called a witch to appear in the mirror. It appeared and jumped into her driving her insane. I tried to lead her in deliverance, but was unsuccessful. I also tried to get her to put her will behind the deliverance by having her call upon the name of Jesus. But she could not say the name of Jesus. This evil spirit blocked her from getting set free. Afterward I learned from this experience that there are evil spirits that block deliverance.

Another time, I was leading several people in breaking ungodly soul ties that they had with people. The demon in one woman prevented her from remembering one of her ex-husband's name. She had been married to him for 5 years. The evil spirit prevented her deliverance from soul ties with him. It was after these incidents that I learned that demons place blocking demons in front of them to protect them from being expelled. I have since addressed this problem when I start deliverance by binding all blocking spirits.

"...The god of this world blinds the minds of the unbelieving so that they may not see the light of the gospel of the glory of Christ who is the image of God. 2 Cor. 4:4 (NASB)

I have also seen the god of this world block the minds of believers so that they would not get set free. In doing deliverance or self-deliverance, it would be wise to start off by binding all spirits of darkness including mind-binding and mind-blocking spirits.

Be sober, be vigilant; because your adversary the devil walks about like a roaring lion, seeking whom he may devour. Resist him, steadfast in the faith, knowing that the same sufferings are experienced by your brotherhood in the world. 1 Peter 5:8-9 (NKJV)

> *Therefore submit to God. Resist the devil and he will flee from you. Draw near to God and He will draw near to you. Cleanse your hands, you sinners; and purify your hearts, you double-minded.* James 4:7-8 (NKJV)

This spiritual warfare is nothing new. The early church battled the same thing. Both of these scriptures remind us that we are to be sober minded and alert, resisting the devil with our wills.

> *Every place that the sole of your foot will tread upon I have given you, as I said to Moses.* Joshua 1:3 (NKJV)

Here we see that the promised land already belonged Moses and Joshua and to the children of Israel. They could stand on the west bank of the Jordon River and look across it and declare that everything on the other side was theirs, given to them by God. And they would be 100% correct doctrinally. But what was actually required of the children of Israel to actually posses their inheritance, was to enter their promise and drive out the inhabitants, foot by foot. In other words, the land was legally theirs, but their enemies were still in actual possession of it.

What we are going to do now is to take the promise of Jesus. In Matthew 15:27, Jesus declares that deliverance is the children's bread. Deliverance belongs to those who are his children, to those that believe in him. Jesus said to those who believe in him:

> *Behold, I give you the authority to trample on serpents and scorpions, and over all the power of the enemy, and nothing shall by any means hurt you.* Luke 10:19 (NKJV)

> *And these signs will follow those who believe: In My name they will cast out demons; they will speak with new tongues; they will take up serpents; and if they drink anything deadly, it will by no means hurt them; they will lay hands on the sick, and they will recover."*

Mark 16:17-18 (NKJV)

*No one can enter a **strong man**'s house and plunder his goods, unless he first binds the strong man. And then he will plunder his house.* Mark 3:27 (NKJV)

In Matthew 18:18 Jesus gives us authority to bind on this earth:

"Assuredly, I say to you, whatever you bind on earth will be bound in heaven, and whatever you loose on earth will be loosed in heaven (NKJV)

So many times I hear believers saying that they are afraid to take their authority and bind and cast out the enemy. If they don't believe they have authority, they are believing a lie that the enemy placed in their heart. Family, trust in the words of Jesus when he said to those who believe in him: *Behold, I give you the authority to trample on serpents and scorpions, and over all the power of the enemy, and nothing shall by any means hurt you.* Luke 10:19 (NKJV) If you are a believer and believe these passages, say Amen.

Sometimes demons come out with a loud voice. (Luke 4:33). There is a lot of breath that is expelled in order to make a loud voice. In "Vines Complete Expository Dictionary" the Greek word for spirit and breath is the same word. "pneuma." When Jesus was casting out evil spirits they came out on a loud voice. (Mark1:26)

It often takes a lot of breath (pneuma), that is, breath/spirit. So in this deliverance, as an act of your will, I will ask you to blow out breath in the name of Jesus to start the process of evil spirits leaving. They don't come out because you blow breath (pnuema) but they come out in the name of Jesus. So I may ask you to blow out breath or to cough, to expel pnuema as an act of your will. I am just getting you into position for deliverance. It helps to get the process started.

When we start deliverance, don't look around the room and say, that demon belongs to that person. Don't look at someone else's problems and don't say, "I never did that or I don't have that, because you may be hindering your own deliverance. Maybe you didn't have that demon, but maybe your ancestors did. (Ex. 20:3-5 and Deut. 23:2).

I have ministered to many people who had a demonic problems such as addiction, lust, prostitution, etc. that came down their generational line. One woman had an incubus spirit that had sex with her and was destroying her marriage. In the name of Jesus Christ, I called out the evil spirit that came into her from the 10th generation, then the 9th, then the 8th, then the 7th and she screamed out and it took me, her husband and several women to restrain her as the evil spirit left her. Later after she was set free, I found out that as far back as she remembered, her family was involved in Santeria Witchcraft. That was the tradition of the family she came from.

Just focus on yourself. You have to get honest with yourself. You have to take a stand against the enemy. If the demon that is being called out sounds or feels like you or part of your personality, then you deal with it now. Put your will behind getting set free. Don't put it off until later or sweep it under the carpet. Write the name of that spirit down and who, where, when or what it makes you think of. That is how it is connected to the spirit that is being called out.

Say this aloud:

Lord Jesus, I believe you are the Son of the living God and you came in the flesh, shed your blood and died on the cross for me to have eternal life, and to heal me and deliver me. I confess that I am a sinner and need your redemption. I receive your shed blood as payment for all my sins. I ask you to forgive me of all my sins. I believe you have forgiven me, I forgive all who have hurt me and I now give my life to you to be my Lord and Savior.

I now take the authority you gave me in Luke 10:19 over all the power of the enemy and the authority in Matt 18:18 to bind the enemy and in Mark 3:27 to bind the strong man.

In the name of Jesus Christ, I now bind the strong man (demon) and all evil spirits at work in my life and any mind blocking spirits and command them to be powerless in Jesus' name. I command any evil spirit that came into me through generational curses to be void of their power in my life. I command every evil spirit that attached themselves to me through ungodly soul ties to be bound and powerless and to be severed from me now in Jesus' name and every demon that was attached to me that came from another person leave me now in Jesus' name. Take a deep breath and blow out. Go! Leave me in Jesus' name.

For God has not given us a spirit of fear, but of power and of love and of a sound mind.
2 Timothy 1:7 (NKJV)

Many of us have a battle over a sound mind. Fear has control and many times you find yourself making decisions based on fear. That is one of the ways the enemy controls us, through fear.

I was working on a woman's pool deck cleaning her pool and she said to me, close the door, lizards might come in." She was terrified of lizards and ran away from one, fell and was in a sling and neck brace because she injured herself. Her fear brought her injury and pain. You can be afraid of many sorts of things, fear of bugs, reptiles, dogs, cats and many other things and the enemy will use that against you.

Remember to speak aloud as you command out the spirits.

In the name of Jesus Christ, I command out of me the spirits of:

Fear and rejection, which is under fear, the one that makes me feel excluded, forgotten, inadequate, left out, overlooked, un- accepted, un-loved, cowardice, doormat, fear of rejection, self rejection.

Take a deep breath and blow it out. Go! Leave me in Jesus' name.

In the name of Jesus Christ, I command out of me:

Fear of authority, fear that distorts authority, that makes me feel helpless when I am around authority, sensitiveness, fear of disapproval, grouchiness, self awareness, self conscious, self pity, stuttering, whining, worry, agitation, anxiety, apprehension, distress, dread, nightmares, terror.

I command you spirits to leave me now in Jesus' name. Take a deep breath and blow it out. Go in Jesus' name.

I want you to take a minute and think about those demons that were called out. I pushed some hot buttons. Pray the following:

Holy Spirit, I ask that you reveal to me where these things came into me. Wait until he shows or reveals through mental images to your mind of people, places or incidents that wounded or hurt you or that seem to be part of your personality.

Now start writing them down. You know what was called out of you, you know what was coming out of you. You know if this hit something that was true. Write it down. It may have been forgotten but now you remember, write it down. If it made you fearful, anxious, self aware, you know the emotion that arose from you when you called these spirits out. Write them down.

Pray, **Holy spirit, I ask you to reveal the source of these things in the name of Jesus.** Now the Lord is showing you where these things came in. He is showing you a snapshot or a picture or you are remembering some incident from those words of deliverance, and it came to your mind and you are now remembering. It might trigger a memory of an ancestor, your grand parents then you know it came into you through an ancestral curse. Perhaps it was a word or a phrase that somebody said to you, then you know that it came in through that. Write them down.

If you are done writing, then hold those papers up to the Lord and say this with me.

Lord, you know where this came in and now I know. Now I command out of me the very demons behind the source of the problem, I command them to leave me now in Jesus' name. Take a deep breath and blow it out. Go! Leave me in Jesus' name.

Whatever you wrote on your paper, whatever the Holy Spirit revealed to you, call it out. The spirit that entered me when...(then fill in the blank...).

Speak aloud: I command you, that one, to go in Jesus' name. Take a deep breath and blow it out, Go! Leave me in Jesus' name.

There you did it. You went to the source – the root of the problem (spider, not the web) and knocked it down. That was self deliverance.

In the name of Jesus Christ, I command out of me the spirits of:

Insecurity, bed wetting, failure, false love, humiliation, inadequacy, ineptness, loneliness, religious fanaticism, shyness, talkativeness, timidity, undependability. I command them to leave me now in Jesus' name. Take a deep breath and blow it out, Go! in Jesus name.

Continue, start writing them down. I know this sounds repetitive but I am teaching you a self deliverance process. You know what you called out of yourself and you know what was coming out of you. As some hot buttons were hit here, write them down.

Pray: Holy Spirit, I ask you to reveal the source of these things in the name of Jesus.

When you are done writing, again hold those papers up to the Lord and say this, **"Lord, you know where this came in and now I know.**

Now I command out of me the demons behind the source of the problem, that causes me to be this way. I command it to leave me now in Jesus name." Take a deep breath and blow it out, Go! Leave in Jesus' name.

When I did this teaching in South Miami, a woman cried out, "I remember when failure entered me. It happened when I failed 2nd grade and I felt so stupid after that. By doing self deliverance, she was set free from feeling like a failure and feeling stupid because she found out where and when the spirit of failure entered her.

Remember, you can call it out by what it makes you feel or does to you, such as, "You, that spirit that makes me feel like such a failure, or makes me feel stupid, go in Jesus' name!" As the Holy Spirit is revealing, jot the word down that is called out and the impression from that word.

In the name of Jesus Christ, I command out of me all spirits of phobia.

Fears, acrophobia, claustrophobia, fear of heights, fear of open places, fear of crowds, fear of people, fear of animals, fear of flying in airplanes, fear of ambulances, fear of babies, fear of being alone, fear of being found out, fear of being discovered, fear of crossing bridges, fear of cancer, fear of cats, fear of dogs, fear of choking, fear of confinement, fear of death, fear of freedom, fear of deliverance, fear of demons, fear of driving a car, fear of elevators, fear of embracement, fear of failure, fear of using a computer, fear of falling, fear of the future, fear of germs, fear of touching a place where someone else touched, fear of sickness, fear of infection, fear of getting hurt, fear of heart attack, fear of hurting people, fear of husbands, fear of wives, fear of insanity, fear of insects, fear of reptiles, fear of snakes, fear of lizards, fear of turtles, fear of intimacy, fear of lightning, fear of losing salvation, fear of loss of identity, fear of making a commitment, fear of marriage, fear of needles, fear of noise, fear of nuclear war, fear of pain, fear of race, fear of responsibility, fear of receiving love, fear of giving love, fear of sex, fear of success, fear of suffocation, fear of darkness, fear of the water.

If I didn't name your fear, you name it and call it out. Say this aloud:, I command out of me the thing that make me afraid of... Now name what makes you afraid.

I command them to leave me now in Jesus' name. Take a deep breath and blow it out, Go in Jesus' name.

Now start writing them down. You know what was called out of you and you know what was coming out of you. Write them down, and the impressions, where those evil spirits came in.

You might have seen a movie, or read a novel or saw something that you wish you had never seen or was told by someone something that struck horror in your heart, that impression never left you. **Pray: Holy Spirit, I ask you to reveal the source of these things in the name of Jesus.**

If you are done writing, then hold those papers up to the Lord and say this: "Lord, you know where this came in and now I know. Now I command out of me the very the demons behind the source of the problem, that caused me to be this way. I command it to leave me now in Jesus' name." I command all those evil spirits that have left me to go and return no more.

Take a deep breath and blow it out. Go in Jesus' name.

Thank you Father for my healing and deliverance. I now surrender to you Lord Jesus all the areas that are now vacant. I give you those areas to rule and reign in. Come Holy Spirit and live in those areas. Amen.

Chapter 10
Levels of Spiritual Warfare

Binding and loosing is the beginning of warfare. The word declares in Deuteronomy 32:30:

How could one chase a thousand, And two put ten thousand to flight,
Unless their Rock had sold them, And the LORD had surrendered them? (NKJV)

The thought I want you to understand is, "*one* will chase away 1,000 and *two* will put 10,000 to flight." This reminds me of what Jesus said in Matthew 18:19:

Again I say to you that if two of you agree on earth concerning anything that they ask, it will be done for them by My Father in heaven. (NKJV)

Jesus gave the body of Christ an amazing gift when he said in Luke 10:19

Behold, I give you the authority to trample on serpents and scorpions, and over all the power of the enemy, and nothing shall by any means hurt you. (NKJV)

One Christian has power over all the power of the enemy, how much more if two Christians pray, three Christians, 10 Christians, 20 Christians. Jesus recognized the satanic kingdom. He claimed in Matthew 12:26:

If Satan casts out Satan, he is divided against himself. How then will his kingdom stand? (NKJV)

Jesus recognized and declared that there is a satanic kingdom and that it exists. It is a shame to most of the Christian churches that they do not recognize that a Satanic kingdom exists today.

Paul tells the church that our struggle is not against flesh and blood. It is against Satan's satanic kingdom and it is divided into four categories of powers.

...For we do not wrestle against flesh and blood, but against **principalities,** *against* **powers,** *against the* **rulers of the darkness of this age,** *against* **spiritual hosts of wickedness in the heavenly places.** *(Cosmos Kratores- foot soldiers Demons)* Ephesians 6:12 (NKJV)

In spiritual warfare, we spend a lot of time battling demons. But I believe if you want to change the atmosphere within you, you must change it around you and above you. So, it makes a lot of sense for us to look at how these 4 categories of darkness operate.

1. Principalities

The first category is **Principalities.** This tells us that there are evil spiritual princes in Satan's kingdom who are assigned to control large portions of the world, nations, states or large political or religious segments of the country. They do this by influencing earthly rulers, kings, presidents, government officials, parliaments, Congress, judges and all who have legal, political influence or rule over regions of the Earth. They do this by assigning a task to rulers of darkness which will be described later.

If Satan can influence these people by his evil prince, he can indirectly rule the people of that region. So, the first segment of Satan's kingdom that we wrestle against is an evil prince of a principality that influence legal rule.

Look to see what evil is going on in your state, what evil exists, what customs and traditions that go on that are against God. Make a list and then you are armed with knowledge on who the evil prince is and what he is doing in your land. Do spiritual warfare against these things on your list and vote people out of office who are not Godly who don't line up with Scripture.

2. Powers

The next category in Satan's kingdom is called **Powers.**

Powers are behind witchcraft, occultism, psychic powers, mental powers, dark arts, transcendental meditation, invisible powers such as "Reki", universal life force. They operate much like electricity operates. Electricity is a real power and a force that is not seen but nevertheless real.

3. Rulers of Darkness

The next category in Satan's kingdom is called **Rulers of Darkness**. They rule regions under the legal authority of the principality. They include governors, county managers, mayors, and they have specific areas of a country or city given over to them to rule. This also includes organized crime, indecent and immoral behavior, gambling, prostitution, adultery, influencing people to justify doing wrong. The devil has power to steal kill and destroy (John 10:10).

4. Spiritual hosts of wickedness in heavenly places

The last one is called **spiritual hosts of wickedness in heavenly places**. There is a blanket of wickedness covering the people of Earth to cause wicked events to happen such as floods, hurricanes, earthquakes, tornadoes, tsunami, tidal waves, forest fires, or any wicked event that would cause theft, death, destruction. There are specific areas on the Earth where wicked events occur. Child sacrifices in Africa have risen to record highs, certain areas given over to homosexuality, the New Age, sorcery, occultism.

It is from this realm that Satan directs his demons and targets not only specific areas but people. It is from this realm Satan assigns demons, as people are given over to evil practices and rebellion against God.

Webster's new American dictionary defines wickedness as evil, sinful, immoral, bad, vicious, harmful, destructive, vile, unpleasant. That is what wickedness produces. Think of these spirits of wickedness as the S. S. of Satan's kingdom.

Hosts of wickedness is what Jesus cast out of people. They are demons that attach to people of the particular region they are assigned to stay in, as in the story of the man with legions of demons found in Mark 5: 10. The demons begged Jesus that He would not send them out of the country. From this we learn that demons are assigned to territories and don't want to leave the territory.

When casting out demons, do not forget to take the war back to the realm from which they were assigned. Command their lines of communications to be confused in heavenly places. Since they were sent as the spiritual hosts of wickedness, bind all spiritual hosts of wickedness when casting out of any demon.

As you can see, these ranks or categories of the satanic kingdom need to be approached in warfare on different levels. In order to do effective warfare against Satan's kingdom, one must know which level of Satan's kingdom they are warning against and concentrate on the effects of that area, not only inside us, but around us and over us. Once an area is targeted, we are to saturate that area with spiritual warfare prayers.

There is another level of warfare spoken about. It is found in our mind.

But I see another law in my members, warring against the law of my mind, and bringing me into captivity to the law of sin which is in my members. O wretched man that I am! Who will deliver me from this body of death? I thank God—through Jesus Christ our Lord! Romans 7:23-25 (NKJV)

Paul writes about the warfare in our mind again in 2 Corinthians 10:3-6:

For though we walk in the flesh, we do not war according to the flesh. For the weapons of our warfare are not carnal but mighty in God for pulling down strongholds, casting down arguments and every high thing that exalts itself against the knowledge of God, bringing every thought into captivity to the obedience of Christ, and being ready to punish all disobedience when your obedience is fulfilled. (NKJV)

Paul writes both to the Romans and to the Corinthians, that there is a war going on in our minds. Thoughts that bring us into captivity; imaginations, arguments, that would cause us to be in disobedience to God.

This level of warfare has been experienced by everyone. When we are called out of darkness into God's kingdom, we join the fight. We must then learn how to fight the war in our minds. If you don't learn, then there is a good chance you will lose ground to the enemy.

Inside of every born again Christian is the potential to win every battle. Many are afraid to war against Satan and his demons and want someone else to fight the fight for them, but God designed you to win.

Behold, I give to you authority to tread on serpents and scorpions, and over all the authority of the enemy. And nothing shall by any means hurt you. Luke 10:19 (MKJV)

So, when we declare and speak things in the name of Jesus Christ to the demonic realm whether they are in the air above us or in our minds, or battling them in the members of our body, we should expect the command to be obeyed.

You cannot reach others for Christ successfully unless you are free yourself. There is an area where we wrestle spiritual forces that have attached themselves to our personal thinking; our minds. In our mind there are personal strongholds that must be dealt with and torn down; concepts, notions, opinions, arguments, knowledge, mindsets, thoughts and imaginations.

Paul says that these things that are called imagination must be cast down or torn down out of our minds and made to come into obedience in Christ. Why? Because the devil wants you to believe and put faith in his lies. He wants you to believe that those things that are in your mind; those unholy imaginations, are **greater** than Christ who is in you.

Whenever God calls you to do great things, the devil will attack your imaginations. You may say to yourself, "I can't do it, I'm too weak, I'm not smart enough, not skilled enough." The devil places negative thoughts in your head so that you will run with them. This is a false image, weak image of self, and when you bow to it, it is idolatry. If you bow to it, you bow to the deity of what brought that thought.

This becomes an altar of fear to a false image and it must be torn down. Also, every place in you where you have practiced sin, you now bow to the demonic altar that is set up inside of you, and when you bow to it, it becomes an idol that you serve (idolatry).

So Family, some spiritual warfare has a lot to do with your mind and and your view of yourself. It may be anger, your tongue, your thought life, attitudes, positions you have taken that are not sound or biblical, that lead to sin and recklessness.

Paul describes an incident of a man who witnessed heaven in 2 Corinthians 12:2-4:

*I know a man in Christ who fourteen years ago— whether in the body I do not know, or whether out of the body I do not know, God knows—such a one was caught up to the third heaven. And I know such a man—whether in the body or out of the body I do not know, God knows — how he was caught up into **Paradise** and heard inexpressible words, which it is not lawful for a man to* *utter.* (NKJV)

Here, Paul tells us possibly about his own adventure, but he really doesn't want to boast, so he says,"he knew a man." This man was caught up into the **third heaven;** Paradise. Paradise is where Jesus is sitting on the throne next to the Father.

Remember what Jesus said to the thief that was next to him on the cross? *Today, you will be with me in paradise* (Luke 23:43). Paradise is as high in the heavens that there is. It is also called by Paul,"the third heaven." So if there is a third heaven, there must be a first and a second heaven also.

The first heaven is the atmosphere above our heads, the sky, clouds, Moon, stars. The second heaven must be beyond that, and the third heaven, Paradise, even further than that. So, where is the warfare that is stated in Ephesians 6 actually located? It must be located here on earth with the world forces of darkness, Satan's ground troops, demons, and powers of darkness, and also in the second heaven above us with the prince of the power of the air (Ephesians 2:2) in spiritual forces of wickedness in heavenly places. These two demonic forces are what we are going to concentrate on.

The prince of the power of the air is located in our immediate atmosphere above our heads in the clouds surrounding the Earth above our cities, counties, states, in countries and further beyond with Principalities in the stars. So, spiritual warfare exists in these spiritual realms.

The prophet Daniel who had been praying and fasting for 3 weeks, fell into a trance and an angel touched him and spoke to him:

> *Then he said to me, "Do not fear, Daniel, for from the first day that you set your heart to understand, and to humble yourself before your God, your words were heard; and I have come because of your words. But the*

prince of the kingdom of Persia withstood me twenty-one days; and behold, Michael, one of the chief princes, came to help me, for I had been left alone there with the kings of Persia. Now I have come to make you understand what will happen to your people in the latter days, for the vision refers to many days yet to come." Daniel 10:12- 14 (NKJV)

Then he said, "Do you know why I have come to you? And now I must return to fight with the prince of Persia; and when I have gone forth, indeed the prince of Greece will come. But I will tell you what is noted in the Scripture of Truth. (No one upholds me against these, except Michael your prince. Daniel 10:20-21 (NKJV)

There was a war in the heavenly realm as soon as Daniel set his heart on understanding. As soon as Daniel started to pray and fast, war started in the heavens and princes of principalities clashed in the air in warfare to prevent the messenger of God in reaching Daniel. In this scripture we come to understand that Satan has his satanic princes over territories, and God assigns His holy prince over territories.

As soon as we start to pray and seek God for an answer, a war starts with principalities. They fight God's holy angels in an unseen battle above our heads. Family, there is warfare above us. We cannot see it but it is happening.

When I was with you daily in the temple, you did not try to seize Me. But this is your hour, and the **power of darkness."** (NKJV) Luke 22:53

Jesus tells them that he has fallen into their hands and the power of darkness. Jesus shows us that there is a power of darkness and Paul tells us in Ephesians 6 that there are powers of darkness and in **Romans 8:38** the things that would separate us from God and in that list of things, there are angels, principalities and **powers.**

God is going to use the church to display His power over

darkness.

> *...to the intent that now the manifold wisdom of God might be made known by the church to the principalities and powers in the heavenly places,* Ephesians 3:10 (NKJV)

> *...which He worked in Christ when He raised Him from the dead and seated Him at His right hand in the heavenly places,*
>
> *21 far above all **principality** and **power** and **might** and **dominion**, and every name that is named, not only in this age but also in that which is to come.* Ephesians 1:20-21 (NKJV)

Now Jesus' work is done and now He sits in Paradise at the right hand of the Father. Now there is no warfare where He sits but we are at war down here. This is why Jesus said in Mark 16:17-18:

> *And these signs will follow those who believe: In My name they will cast out demons; they will speak with new tongues; they will take up serpents; and if they drink anything deadly, it will by no means hurt them; they will lay hands on the sick, and they will recover."* (NKJV)

Even though Jesus describes what a believer's authority is to look like, many are unaware of deliverance and the existence of the warfare and the strategies, schemes, and plots of the enemy. Many who are unaware of spiritual warfare have fallen and have not fulfilled their calling because they were unaware.

> *My people are destroyed for lack of knowledge. Because you have rejected knowledge, I also will reject you from being priest for Me; Because you have forgotten the law of your God, I also will forget your children.* Hosea 4:6 (NKJV)

We are not to sit around and wait for our destruction and

the destruction of our children, but we are to take the war to the enemy's backyard. We are supposed to learn scripture and apply it to our lives. As Paul tells us in Romans 15:4, *For whatever things were written before were written for our learning,* (NKJV). First of all remember that these things were written that we and our children would not be destroyed and second they were written for our learning. God wants us to know and be aware of what could destroy us. We are in a real war and the Lord God is a man of war.

> Moses and the children of Israel sang this song to the LORD, and spoke, saying in Exodus 15:1-3 (NKJV):
>
> "*I will sing to the LORD,*
>
> *For He has triumphed gloriously! The horse and its rider*
>
> *He has thrown into the sea!*
>
> *2 The LORD is my strength and song, And He has become my salvation; He is my God, and I will praise Him;*
>
> *My father's God, and I will exalt Him.*
>
> **The LORD is a man of war; The LORD is His name.**

God is a man of war. We have seen this many times in the Bible where He supernaturally destroys armies and nations. In this scripture we just read, Pharaoh's servants chased Israel through the parted Red Sea and somewhere before reaching the other side, God cause confusion on the Egyptians chariot wheels to swerve with difficulty.

In the previous chapter, Exodus 14:25, the Egyptians cried out, "*Let us flee from the face of Israel, for the Lord fights for them against the Egyptians."* (NKJV)

Throughout the Bible, you will see that God has not stopped fighting for his children when they are faced by their enemies. He also expects his children to stand up to the fight, and He trains us for the battle.

Psalm 144:1 (NKJV)

Blessed be the LORD my Rock, Who trains my hands for war, And my fingers for battle—

God is the best trainer and when he trains his children for battle, they are then to train the ones under them. That is what I am doing here. I have been trained by the Lord and now I am training you the way I have been trained.

*When Abram heard that his relative (Lot) had been taken captive, he led out his **trained** men, born in his house, three hundred and eighteen, and went in pursuit as far as Dan.* Genesis 14:14 (NASB)

Abram raised an army of trained and armed soldiers and had complete and total victory. Jesus said in Matthew 10:34 (NKJV), "*Do not think that I came to bring peace on earth. I did not come to bring peace but a sword.* Jesus brought a **sword to this Earth. He brought war**. He cast out demons. Then he instructs us to bind the strongman and then plunder his house. (Matt 12:28) These are all very violent acts of war.

Christ in Christianity is warlike. Most churches do not understand this aspect of Jesus. this is why there is much spiritual decay and disarray in their congregations. Jesus saves souls by bringing people into repentance and offering them a choice to come back to the Father so that they would turn from their sins. He did miracles, healed people, and cast out demons by the Holy Spirit. That is all part of real warfare – to establish freedom for people.

Preaching salvation is fishing for the souls of men, and the casting out of demons is fighting for the souls of men. They are two different things, but both are considered in warfare to bring people into a right standing with God.

Paul writes in 2 Timothy 4:7 (NKJV), *I have fought the good fight, I have finished the race, I have kept the faith.*

I pray that the Holy Spirit places this on your heart today to do the same. Don't let anything control you, anything that is in your life that does not glorify God through Jesus Christ. Don't mix Jesus with anything. And don't let anything rule you that is not of the Holy Spirit.

We are at war with a real enemy who wants to steal kill and destroy us (John 10:10). The enemy wants to take you to hell to burn in the lake of fire forever. Spiritual warfare means that we are at war with evil spirits. I spoke earlier of warfare that is found in a different realm in our mind. (Daniel chapter 10 and Ephesians chapter 6 and in Second Corinthians 10). These evil spirits aren't visible but you can witness the effects they have on your and other people's lives.

Spiritual warfare is a battle between the people who are loyal to God and a network of evil spirits that are loyal to Satan. It is the warfare between these two kingdoms that is fought in the spiritual realm.

As I said earlier, there is warfare in the heavenlies. We can bring warfare to the skies and declare our warfare into the skies as Joshua did.

Then Joshua spoke to the LORD in the day when the LORD delivered up the Amorites before the children of Israel, and he said in the sight of Israel:

"Sun, stand still over Gibeon; And Moon, in the Valley of Aijalon." So the sun stood still, and the moon stopped, till the people had revenge upon their enemies. Joshua 10:12-13 (NKJV)

Joshua, a man filled with the calling and destiny of God said boldly in the sight of Israel, **Sun and Moon, stand still.** He didn't want the day to end until **all** his enemies had been defeated. In Spiritual warfare, we must be as bold as Joshua was and declare in the sight of all men. With authority, we are to war in the heavens as well as on earth.

Here are several reasons why we should fight spiritual forces of darkness. We fight spiritual warfare because Jesus fought spiritual warfare.

1. Destroy the devil's works

> *He who sins is of the devil, for the devil has sinned from the beginning. For this purpose the Son of God was manifested, that He might <u>destroy the works of the devil</u>.* 1 John 3:8 (NKJV)

> *Most assuredly, I say to you, he who believes in Me, the works that I do he will do also; and greater works than these he will do, because I go to My Father.* John 14:12 (NKJV)

Jesus came to <u>destroy the works of the devil</u> and we who believe on him shall also do his works and destroy the works of the devil because we are supposed to be doing the things that Jesus did.

2. Put off the old man

> *...that you put off, concerning your former conduct, the old man which **grows corrupt** according to the deceitful lusts, and be renewed in the spirit of your mind, and that you put on the new man which was created according to God, in true righteousness and holiness.* Ephesians 4:22-24 (NKJV)

We should fight spiritual forces of darkness because it is a daily battle to change the old man's way of thinking into the renewed thinking of the new man in Christ.

3. Escape the devil's snares

> *...and that they (WE) may come to their senses and escape the snare of the devil, having been taken captive by him to do his will.* 2 Timothy 2:26 (NKJV)

4. To open people's eyes

*... to **open their eyes**, in order to turn them from darkness to light, and from the power of Satan to God, that they may receive forgiveness of sins and an inheritance among those who are sanctified by faith in Me.'* Act. 26:17-18 (NKJV)

We should fight spiritual forces of darkness is to free sinners, bringing them into the Kingdom.

5. We are to minister the Gospel to the brokenhearted, the captives, the infirmed and the oppressed because Jesus did.

"The Spirit of the LORD is upon Me, because He has anointed Me to preach the gospel to the poor; he has sent Me to heal the brokenhearted, to proclaim liberty to the captives And recovery of sight to the blind, to set at liberty those who are oppressed; Luke 4:18 (NKJV)

6. To maintain our victory.

Fight the good fight of faith, lay hold on eternal life, to which you were also called and have confessed the good confession in the presence of many witnesses. 1 Timothy 6:12 (NKJV)

At the very end of time, it is interesting to note who is thrown into the lake of fire.

*The **devil**, who deceived them, was cast into the lake of fire and brimstone where the **beast** and the **false prophet** are. And they will be tormented day and night forever and ever.* Revelation 20:10 (NKJV)

We know the devil (Satan) who reigns over the demonic kingdom is thrown in the lake of fire and the beast in Rev. 20 who waged war against the saints and the other beast who demands worship and places 666 on all people, he is also thrown in the lake of fire, but then we see that the false prophet is one of the three who is thrown into the lake of fire. Why, you ask? Because he is the satanic counterfeit of the true biblical office of prophet.

When God spoke to men in the Old Covenant, He chose men to communicate his message. God spoke through man, to the people. In the New Covenant, God speaks prophetically through the Holy Spirit directly to the people.

It makes sense to me that there is a false prophetic spirit at work in the heavens that wage war against the human race by bringing misinformation, false information accusation and deception. It also makes sense to me that this evil spirit would be under the evil prince of **principalities** that influence legal rule.

Throughout the old and the New Testament, we find references of false prophets who deceived and turned Israel away from the truth. Some examples are the magicians of Pharaoh. They had great influence directly under Pharaoh's power. Another example is found in Acts 13: 6-11. There we can see characteristics of a false prophet:

*Now when they had gone through the island to Paphos, they found a certain **sorcerer**, a **false prophet**, a Jew whose name was Bar-Jesus, who was with the proconsul, Sergius Paulus, an intelligent man. This man called for Barnabas and Saul and sought to hear the word of God. But Elymas the sorcerer (for so his name is translated) withstood them, **seeking to turn the proconsul away from the faith**. Then Saul, who also is called Paul, filled with the Holy Spirit, looked intently at him and said, "O **full of all deceit** and **all fraud**, you **son of the devil**, you **enemy of all righteousness**, will you not cease **perverting the straight ways of the Lord**? And now, indeed, the hand of the Lord is upon you, and you shall be blind, not seeing the sun for a time. "And immediately a dark mist fell on him, and he went around seeking someone to lead him by the hand.* Acts 13: 6-11 (NKJV)

This spirit of false prophet comes from the prince of principalities and attacks ministries and ministers such as Moses and later we see attacking Paul and Silias. The false prophet's job given to him with false authority, is to pass false judgment and evil statements over believers who have genuine ministries. In addition, he operates as the accuser of the brethren, the spirit of error, heresy, witchcraft, deception lying, mind control, religious spirits, slander, pride, back-biting strife, dissension, division jealousy and maligning the flock.

Let's get ready for warfare. Using the New King James Version, let us review these key verses:

> **Matthew 12:29** ...*or how can one enter a strong man's house and plunder his goods, unless he first binds the strong man? And then he will plunder his house.*
>
> **Matthew 18:19** *"Again I say to you that if two of you agree on earth concerning anything that they ask, it will be done for them by My Father in heaven.*
>
> **Luke 10:19** *Behold, I give you the authority to trample on serpents and scorpions, and over all the power of the enemy, and nothing shall by any means hurt you.*
>
> **Mark 16:17** *And these signs will follow those who believe: In My name they will cast out demons;*
>
> **Ephesians 6:12** ...*for we do not wrestle against flesh and blood, but against **principalities,** against **powers,** against the **rulers of the darkness of this age**, against **spiritual hosts of wickedness in the heavenly places***

Speak aloud the following:

Dear Lord, In the name of Jesus we take the authority You gave us and bind the strongman to plunder his house. We agree with your word that whatever we ask shall be done.

We now command all **Principalities, Powers, Rulers of Darkness of this age, and all spiritual host of wickedness in heavenly places** to be bound and powerless. We command you not to send aid to each other. We command confusion upon your lines of communications and against your hold over regions, states and for your cities to be up rooted and your domains, princes, principalities, powers, rulers of darkness, spiritual hosts of wickedness, to be cast down in defeat and for all your chariot wheels to be stuck in the mud and for the waves of calamity to fall upon you in judgment, for we declare your defeat and total destruction.

Heavenly Father, we pray in agreement and in the name of Jesus for You to send forth your princes of war to overthrow our spiritual enemies in Jesus' name.

In the name of Jesus Christ, we pull down and expel:

Witchcraft, Jezebel, Anti- Christ spirit, occultism, drugs, false prophet, gambling, fleshly seduction, prostitution, all the spiritual king pins of organized crime, bribes and political corruption, lust for money, lust for power. We sever every tentacle of your influence over every human under your domain and command and declare your power void and shut off in the name of Jesus Christ.

In the name of Jesus Christ, I command out of me the spirit of:

False prophecy, sorcery, spiritual corruption that has blinded my eyes, that has prevented me from hearing and seeing the truth of the gospel, that turns me away from the faith, that fill me with deceit and fraud, enemy of righteousness, you who perverts the straight ways of the

Lord, Come out of me in the name of Jesus Christ.

Take a deep breath and blow it out. Go! Leave in the name of Jesus.

In the name of Jesus Christ, I command out of me all evil spirits that make me:

Pass false judgment and evil statements over believers with genuine ministries, accuser of the brethren, the spirit of error, heresy, witchcraft, deception lying, mind control, religious spirits, slander, pride, backbiting strife, dissension, division jealousy and maligning the flock and spirits that hate godly people. Come out of me in the name of Jesus Christ.

Take a deep breath and blow it out. Go in the name of Jesus!

In the name of Jesus Christ, I command out of me:

Error, mind power, psychic power, soul power, occultism, house of the devil, spirit of counterfeit healing, evil spirits that manifest from energy, sound, vibration, light, smoke, feathers, prince of the power of the air, disobedience, rebellion, prince of darkness, queen of darkness, Satanism, vampires, drinkers of blood, anti-Christ, hatred of God, hatred of man, worship of demons, worship of science, worship of religion.

Come out of me in the name of Jesus Christ. Take a deep breath and blow it out. Go in the name of Jesus!

In the name of Jesus Christ, I command out of me spirits of:

The love of power, of position, of money, vanity, self-love, egotistical pride, of orgies, ritualistic sex, captivation, magic, bride of Satan, mediums, spiritualist, spiritual prostitution, murder, abortion, child sacrifice, human sacrifice, Molech, death, familiar spirits, spirit guides, consulting with the dead, spell casting, spirits of wizards, warlocks, Masons, Grand Marshals, the spirit of death, accidents, household gods, Reiki – universal life energy force, Kabala, charmers, serpents and scorpion spirits, reptile spirits, spirits of Santeria witchcraft, Elegua, Obatala, Shango, Oshun, Babalu Aye, Ogun, Orunla and the spirits of Palero Macumba, Palo Mayombe.

Go in the name of Jesus Christ. Take a deep breath and blow out. Go in the name of Jesus Christ.

In the name of Jesus Christ, I command out of me:

Rejection, self- rejection, rejection of others, rejection of God, rejection of his statues, rejection of his ways, rejection of his people, bitterness, resentment, rebellion against God, hatred, anti- God, aggression against God, aggression against God's law, anti- salvation by Jesus Christ, anti-Bible, Antichrist, anti-anointing, un- forgiveness toward self, un-forgiveness toward others, un- forgiveness towards God, temper, violence, rage, anger, retaliation, murder, abortion, suicide, Come out of me in the name of Jesus Christ.

Everyone take a deep breath and blow it out. Go! Leave me in the name of Jesus.

In the name of Jesus Christ, I command out of me:

Rebellion, self-willed, self-worship, self-righteous, haughty, vain, hardhearted, stubbornness, disobedience, anti-submission, strife in the family, quarreling, fighting, physical and verbal abuse, demonic domination, dominance, using words or sex to control others, self-idolatry, idol worship, witchcraft, deception, lies, vain imaginations, lust of the eyes, love of self, insecurity, conquest in lust for flesh, material things, self-gratification, the spirit that declines my morals, decay, rot, adultery, fornication, sodomy, demonic sex, frigidity, perverted sex, pornography, homosexuality.

Come out of me in the name of Jesus Christ. Take a deep

breath and blow it out. Go! Leave me in the name of Jesus.

In the name of Jesus Christ, I command out of me:
Spirit of divorce, separation, escape, depression, despair, discouragement, defeat, gloom, heaviness, spirit of unbelief, occult, drugs, ESP, hypnotism, fortune telling, divination, witchcraft, soul travel, deception, slander, back biting, accusation, arrogance, the spirit that makes me exalt myself up above God. Come out of me in the name of Jesus Christ.

Take a deep breath and blow it out. Go in the name of Jesus

.In the name of Jesus Christ, I command out of me:

Foolishness, self-hatred, idolatry, serving self, childlike self- willed, distraction, wariness, betrayal, hatred of husband, hatred of wife, disrespect, spirit of independence, marriage breaking spirits, anti-restoration, spirits that give bad advice, attention seeker, bestiality, blasphemy, blabbermouth, cruelty, condemnation, self- destruction, dread, false beliefs, false religion, false compassion, false doctrine, false front, falsehood, fake, fear of failure, paranoia, overly sensitive, gluttony, loss of love; loving friends, money, possessions in place of loving God, twisted religious beliefs.

Take a deep breath and blow it out. Go in the name of Jesus.

Lord Jesus, I now give you the areas where these demons were ruling. And I now ask You to rule and reign in these areas. I surrender my whole being to you for you to be Lord. Come Holy Spirit take the place of these demons that were cast out and fill me with your power to resist the enemy. Amen.

Dear Family, I hope these pages have been helpful and useful to you. I pray that you have been set free in many areas of your life. I also pray for your continual growth in the Lord Jesus Christ and may you draw closer to the Father because of your new found freedom. Many of the topics discussed in this book may evoke a desire to know more about them. I and my (late) father have addressed many of the problems and questions in our other books. You will find a list of them and how to order them on the following pages.

Blessings, Frank Marzullo, Jr.

BOOKS by Frank Marzullo, Sr.
(Books range from $6.00-$18.00)
- Manual for the Deliverance Worker
- Battle for your Mind
- Breaking the Curses of Deut 27-28
- Breaking Satan's Bondage--What Spirits Motivate You?
- Can a Demon Have a Christian?
- Conquering Anger--Overcoming the Enemy Within
- Conquering Giants in Your Promised Land
- Deliverance from Spirits Named in the Bible
- Doing the Works of Jesus
- Dying to Self
- Eight Keys to Spiritual & Physical Health
- Escaping Satan's Prison
- Fighting & Winning the Spiritual Battle
- Healing Broken Hear & Wounded Spirit
- Spirit of the Bride of Satan
- Unforgiveness--Obstacle to Healing
- Victory over Demonic Spirits
- Witchcraft and the Spirit of Jezebel
- Reaching Your Potential
- Sound Mind Not Fear
- Power in the Blood of Jesus
- Power in the Spoken Word Wounded Spirit
- How to Pray for Healing
- Incubus & Succubus Spirits
- Loneliness, the Killer

BOOKS IN SPANISH
(collections from above list):
- La Plentitud de Una Vita Abundante
- Llaves Para Ministrar Liberacion y Sanidad
- Manual de Liberacion
- Estrategicas Biblicas para Destruir Reino de Satanas
- Victoria Sobre Los Espiritus Malignos

BOOKS by Jill Marzullo
- Our Hope is Anchored in the Cross of Christ

BOOKS by Frank Marzullo, Jr.
- Unbelief an Obstacle to Miracles
- Familiar Spirits
- Serpent and Scorpion Spirits
- Spiritual Warfare Now – Fighting for the Souls of Men
- Spirits that Attach to Leaders and Attack the Church
- Overthrowing the Kingdom of Darkness with Violence
- How Fear Affects our Decisions
- Canceling Satan's Contracts and Assignments
- Judging Others Without Pride
- Four Ways the Enemy can Get In
- Exposing False Salvation with Repentance
- Exposing the Spirits of Rejection and Condemnation

Cd's of select messages are available by request

To listen to Frank's Audio and Video Archives please visit our website www.spiritualwarfarenow.com

You may order online at our website
www.spiritualwarfarenow.com
Or you may contact us at: (386)736-2820
Email: marzullo@bellsouth.net

Frank Marzullo, Jr. is available for seminars on healing and deliverance. Please call, email or visit our web site for more information

NOTES

NOTES

NOTES

IN THE RAYS OF LIGHT

LIVING THE QURAN
THROUGH
THE LIVING QURAN

THE STAR

SŪRAH AL-NAJM

Written by Shaykh Muḥsin Qarā'atī
Translated by Saleem Bhimji

Edited by Arifa Hudda

ISBN 978-1-927930-45-8

Commentary of Sūrah al-Najm
A Translation from *Tafsīr Nūr*
Written by Shaykh Muḥsin Qarā'atī

Translated by Saleem Bhimji
Edited by Arifa Hudda

Published by Islamic Publishing House

www.iph.ca · iph@iph.ca

Cover Design and Layout by Saleem Bhimji for the Islamic Publishing House

Copyright © 2023 by Islamic Publishing House

All Rights Reserved

Without limiting the rights under copyright reserved above, no part of this publication may be reproduced, stored in, or introduced into a retrieval system, or transmitted, in any form, or by any means (electronic, mechanical, photocopying, recording, or otherwise), without the prior written permission of both the copyright owner and the publishers of this book.